Collaborative Grant-Seeking

PRACTICAL GUIDES FOR LIBRARIANS

About the Series

This innovative series written and edited for librarians by librarians provides authoritative, practical information and guidance on a wide spectrum of library processes and operations.

Books in the series are focused, describing practical and innovative solutions to a problem facing today's librarian and delivering step-by-step guidance for planning, creating, implementing, managing, and evaluating a wide range of services and programs.

The books are aimed at beginning and intermediate librarians needing basic instruction/guidance in a specific subject and at experienced librarians who need to gain knowledge in a new area or guidance in implementing a new program/service.

About the Series Editor

The **Practical Guides for Librarians** series was conceived by and is edited by M. Sandra Wood, MLS, MBA, AHIP, FMLA, Librarian Emerita, Penn State University Libraries.

M. Sandra Wood was a librarian at the George T. Harrell Library, the Milton S. Hershey Medical Center, College of Medicine, Pennsylvania State University, Hershey, PA, for over thirty-five years, specializing in reference, educational, and database services. Ms. Wood worked for several years as a development editor for Neal-Schuman Publishers.

Ms. Wood received an MLS from Indiana University and an MBA from the University of Maryland. She is a fellow of the Medical Library Association and served as a member of MLA's Board of Directors from 1991 to 1995. Ms. Wood is founding and current editor of *Medical Reference Services Quarterly*, now in its thirty-fifth volume. She also was founding editor of the *Journal of Consumer Health on the Internet* and the *Journal of Electronic Resources in Medical Libraries* and served as editor/coeditor of both journals through 2011.

Titles in the Series

1. *How to Teach: A Practical Guide for Librarians* by Beverley E. Crane
2. *Implementing an Inclusive Staffing Model for Today's Reference Services* by Julia K. Nims, Paula Storm, and Robert Stevens
3. *Managing Digital Audiovisual Resources: A Practical Guide for Librarians* by Matthew C. Mariner
4. *Outsourcing Technology: A Practical Guide for Librarians* by Robin Hastings
5. *Making the Library Accessible for All: A Practical Guide for Librarians* by Jane Vincent

Collaborative Grant-Seeking

A Practical Guide for Librarians

Bess G. de Farber

PRACTICAL GUIDES FOR LIBRARIANS, NO. 24

ROWMAN & LITTLEFIELD
Lanham • Boulder • New York • London

Published by Rowman & Littlefield
A wholly owned subsidary of The Rowman & Littlefield Publishing Group, Inc.
4501 Forbes Boulevard, Suite 200, Lanham, Maryland 20706
www.rowman.com

Unit A, Whitacre Mews, 26-34 Stannary Street, London SE11 4AB

British Library Cataloguing in Publication Information Available

Library of Congress Cataloging-in-Publication Data

Names: de Farber, Bess G., 1956– author.
Title: Collaborative grant-seeking : a practical guide for librarians / Bess G. de Farber.
Description: Lanham : Rowman & Littlefield, [2016] | Series: Practical guides for librarians ;
no. 24 | Includes bibliographical references and index.
Identifiers: LCCN 2015042494 (print) | LCCN 2016004485 (ebook) | ISBN 9781442263260
(cloth : alk. paper) | ISBN 9781442263277 (pbk. : alk. paper) | ISBN 9781442263284
(electronic)
Subjects: LCSH: Proposal writing in library science–United States–Handbooks, manuals, etc.
| Library fund raising–United States–Handbooks, manuals, etc. | Proposal writing for grants–
United States–Handbooks, manuals, etc. | Fund raising–Teamwork–United States.
Classification: LCC Z683.2.U6 D38 2016 (print) | LCC Z683.2.U6 (ebook) |
DDC 025.1/1–dc23 LC record available at http://lccn.loc.gov/2015042494

♾™ The paper used in this publication meets the minimum requirements of American
National Standard for Information Sciences—Permanence of Paper for Printed Library
Materials, ANSI/NISO Z39.48-1992.

Printed in the United States of America

Contents

List of Tables

Preface

In most libraries across the country, grant-seeking activities are sporadic or completely absent. In light of the untold benefits to be garnered—not just financial—why are so many librarians missing these valuable opportunities? The reasons could be many. If you are a librarian you might say that you do not have the luxury of sufficient time required to do this work. Or that grantsmanship training was nonexistent in library school. Or that you are inhibited by the level of competition for grant funding. Or that any number of other circumstances prevent you from pursuing these activities. If some of this line of thinking rings true, you will find helpful guidance on the pages ahead.

The intent of *Collaborative Grant-Seeking: A Practical Guide for Librarians* is to prevail over these obstacles and provide you with the know-how to build a successful grant-seeking program in your library. For many reasons, including the following, grant-seeking can and should be a collaborative activity that routinely takes place in libraries:

1. Librarians have the capacity to be very successful grant-seekers. Consider all the various assets that are accessible to you: knowledge about online searching, immediate access to information resources on virtually every subject on earth, and the inherent credibility and legitimacy of librarians and libraries as potential grant partners or grant applicants. Many sponsors award grant funds to libraries and some do so exclusively.
2. Librarians serve grant-seekers who are their patrons; knowing about the ins and outs of grantsmanship can enhance customer service to these patrons.
3. Historically, other types of nonprofit and educational organizations have incorporated grant-seeking and grants management as indispensable programs for acquiring funds that support research, facilities, outreach programs, and more. By not participating fully, librarians are missing out on many funding opportunities to support their unfulfilled wish lists.

Another reason why librarians should be more engaged in grant-seeking is that this activity provides a perfect method for learning how to develop new projects. Grant applications in and of themselves are excellent tools for creating something special from a simple idea. An application for funding can be turned into a "container" to be filled with information that defines a project. The progression of the questions provided by the sponsor in its guidelines can guide librarians, their project teams, and their partners as they plan their proposed project. Depending on the quality of the guidelines, librarians may find that no other framework is as effective for planning future programs, facilities, or digitization projects.

⑥ Organization

Collaborative Grant-Seeking: A Practical Guide for Librarians presents seven chapters that progress from information about the history of funding for libraries to detailed instructions on how to prepare fundable grant applications with your project team and partners. Each chapter provides step-by-step guidelines that have been proven successful for librarians and other library employees in developing proficiencies related to all types of grant-seeking activities. Actual excerpts from awarded grant applications help to illustrate successful ways of conveying both simple and complex ideas to those who will be reviewing your future applications.

Chapter 1, "The Pursuit of Grant Funds," describes the relationship between the significant traditions of philanthropic and governmental funding, and the support of libraries in the United States. It posits a rationale for why libraries should be in the grant-seeking business.

Chapter 2, "Collaborative Concepts and Practical Approaches," examines the four different ways to combine forces with project team members and partners to identify the contributions of others toward completing a proposed project. Methods for finding partners and learning about potentially hidden community assets that can add value to your proposed project are featured. A sample agenda for convening partners at the first grant project development meeting sets out the initial steps of securing buy-in and partner contributions for the proposed project.

Chapter 3, "Creating a Library Grant-Seeking Program," details each process for establishing an internal "mini-grant" program in libraries. This successful professional development program, unlike other internally funded library grant programs, seeks to train librarians and library employees in the proficiencies of grant project development and writing. From brainstorming methods to mentorship, the information in this chapter can serve as a model for supporting the professionalization of grant-writing activities in libraries.

Chapter 4, "Searching for External Grant Opportunities," shares a variety of strategies and sources for identifying grant-funding agencies that support libraries, including how to organize these opportunities to be useful resources.

Chapter 5, "Ways to Grow a Culture of Grantsmanship," establishes the means by which libraries can make collaborative grant-seeking into routine activities within their standard operations. This chapter presents ways to share information about grant opportunities, and describes practical steps for offering meaningful training sessions to librarians and interested library employees.

Chapter 6, "Strategies for Completing Application Components," removes the mysteries of how to go about organizing the grant application requirements and the project team to develop and write a fundable grant application, while following a sponsor's guidelines.

Chapter 7, "Grant-Writing Tips and Potential Errors to Avoid," offers recommendations for establishing credibility with your future grant proposal reviewers. These "dos" and "don'ts" will eliminate the guesswork when it comes time to complete the grant application contents. Years of trial and error may be avoided by learning these techniques that can be applied immediately.

The world in which libraries currently operate continues to evolve at a rate that may be faster than a librarian's capacity to respond. One way to navigate these changes is to find mechanisms that enable libraries to meet new needs, and to take advantage of new opportunities. Grant-seeking activities have the potential to be a library's most valuable tool in this pursuit.

Acknowledgments

Becoming a professional grant-writer or grant-manager was not something that I envisioned for myself, but it happened. Peggy MacLeod, the executive director of the Pinellas County Arts Council in the 1980s, assured me that if I were to accept the director of grants and organization services position at the Palm Beach County Cultural Council, there would always be jobs available to me in the world of grants. Much credit for my career in this field—and for the existence of this book—should go to Peggy for her insight. The truest ally and accomplished grant-writer, Stephanie Haas, emeritus librarian of the University of Florida, deserves acknowledgment for her unwavering beliefs in my abilities. University of Florida librarian LeiLani Freund's mantra for the past two years has been "Write your book"—her authorship mentoring has been of great support. Had it not been for M. Sandra Wood, a consummate librarian and my editor at Rowman & Littlefield who invited me to submit the book proposal on this subject, I would never have thought to do such a thing. Her knowledgeable expertise and guidance have been absolutely indispensable. And to Glen Boecher, my in-house editor who protected Sandy from having to plow through my many streams of consciousness . . . a sincere and heart-filled thank-you.

The Pursuit of Grant Funds

A Brief History of Funding and Libraries

THE DEVELOPMENT OF LIBRARIES in the United States has been inextricably tied to the inception of philanthropic giving, and to the origins of government support for the benefit of communities. Libraries have played an essential role in the founding of the nonprofit sector, and in the establishment of government funding to support the quality of life of its citizens, and the collective needs of society as a whole.

The oldest nonprofit organization, and the oldest institution of higher education in the country, is Harvard University, established in 1636. Its namesake, John Harvard, bequeathed his library containing four hundred books along with half of his estate to the college in 1638 (Harvard University, 2015). Harvard, of course, was keenly aware that the heart of any academic institution must be its library, and that without one, a college cannot perform its educational mandate. The gift of his library essentially represents the birth of the nonprofit charitable sector in the United States.

Prior to the American Revolution, most books in the colonies were imported from England. Although publishing in the new nation grew considerably in the decades after 1776, academic libraries generally continued to be comparatively small operations well into the twentieth century, containing mainly volumes on theology, the classics, and standard treatises on philosophy, logic, and history (Weiner, 2005).

In 1783, James Madison proposed, unsuccessfully, that one of the very first appropriations of the new government's funds be used to create a congressional library (Library of Congress, 2006b). The Library of Congress was eventually established in 1800 through legislation signed by President John Adams, granting $5,000 "for the purchase of such books as may be necessary for the use of Congress," that also established the seat of government in Washington, D.C., the new capital. The funds were used to purchase a total of 740 books and three maps from London, England (Library of Congress, 2006a).

In the early 1800s, the federal government began the practice of offering grants to state and local governments, primarily in the form of land, or proceeds from the sale of land, to be used partially for "the encouragement of learning" and the establishment of colleges and universities. It was not until 1862, however, that President Lincoln signed into law the Morrill Act, sponsored by Vermont congressman Justin Morrill and officially titled "An Act Donating Public Lands to the Several States and Territories Which May Provide Colleges for the Benefit of Agriculture and the Mechanic Arts." Pursuant to this piece of legislation, each state was given thirty thousand acres of federal land for each member of the state's congressional delegation. The states then sold the land and used the proceeds to establish public colleges and academic libraries that focused on agriculture and the mechanical arts. Sixty-nine colleges were established by these land grants (Library of Congress, 2015). With these public investments for creating academic facilities came the inevitable need to continue supporting the country's first academic libraries.

Harvard and Yale established endowments to operate their libraries during this period, enabling the solicitation of gifts to establish a more stable foundation for operations and building collections. On or near many college campuses, literary society libraries were created and assumed an important role in supplementing the collections available to students and faculty. These libraries were supported by membership dues and donations, and their books typically included fiction, drama, history, political science, biography, and travel. They declined toward the end of the nineteenth century when natural sciences became more prominent in college curricula and the growth of endowments and funding for college libraries increased (Weiner, 2005).

The establishment of public libraries was slow to take hold during the country's first century; though by 1876, free public libraries, invariably supported by local taxes, numbered 188, in addition to the many more school libraries. That centennial year is generally considered to be the beginning of the modern public library movement, significant for the introduction of the Dewey Decimal System, invented by Melvin Dewey, and the founding of the American Library Association (Jaeger et al., 2013).

The following decades witnessed a sharp increase in philanthropic donations, most notably by the steel magnate Andrew Carnegie. Carnegie gave more than $41 million to 1,420 towns between 1886 and 1919 to establish public libraries. During these years libraries came to embrace expanded roles in their communities, offering a broad range of educational and cultural activities such as exhibits, lectures, meeting spaces for community groups, and services specifically designed to benefit discrete populations such as immigrants and children (Jaeger et al., 2013).

In the twentieth century, public libraries became inexorably involved in political issues beyond the perennial efforts to sustain or augment their share of local tax revenues. Due to the libraries' increased importance to communities and the nation as a whole, and to the nature of the core and expanded services provided, they were often close to the center of controversy on issues surrounding wartime propaganda, censorship, civil rights, and social services in general.

The year 1956 brought the federal government's first foray into funding for public libraries with the passage of the Library Services Act (LSA). This was followed by the enactment of the Library Services and Construction Act in 1964, which later became the Library Services and Technology Act (LSTA). Appropriations under these federal statutes, however, have been relatively modest, comprising far less than 1 percent of total library funding (Jaeger et al., 2013).

Historically, public libraries have depended on local tax dollars for their general operating budgets; academic libraries have relied primarily on state appropriations or endowments. This historical trend has continued to the present time. Libraries might be seen to have lived a sheltered existence in that respect. Up until this century, there had never been a serious threat to these core funding sources. Government support and private donations previously had enabled them to thrive.

The fallout from the economic crisis of 2008 has been felt in every corner of the nation, including libraries. More recently, library funding, particularly in the public sector, is no longer secure; public libraries, including public academic libraries, have found themselves competing with core governmental services such as police, fire, and education for diminishing tax dollars (Coffman, 2006). Many libraries saw crippling budget cuts as both state and local appropriations were drastically reduced (Kelly, 2011). Although current signs may indicate that library funding is in recovery (Schwartz, 2013), the point has been clearly made that library budgets are far too vulnerable to the unpredictable vagaries of economic and political trajectories.

Other than libraries, most nonprofit and government entities have always had to rely on grants revenues to sustain and grow their operations and services. Libraries have not had the need to seek grant support because of their past stable funding sources. Now that library administrators have experienced uncertainties in their traditional revenue sources, the time could be right to seriously consider the long-term benefits of establishing grant-seeking programs to diversify and enhance their financial resources.

An Overview of Grantsmanship and Grant-Seeking

Many people have the impression that writing and submitting grant proposals is a simple matter. The TV commercials where the "used car salesman" peddles a phone book–sized directory of untapped grants resources might be seen as trivializing the important and life-changing field of grant-seeking and grants management. It might seem that grant money is essentially "free" money—well, it is not exactly free; you have to work for it.

Converting an idea into a story about pursuing an opportunity, or the need to fill a gap, solve a problem, or research new ways to do these things is not easy, but it can be learned. This work has the potential to be extremely creative and rewarding. The process of producing a fundable grant proposal offers a chance to organize words and convey related financial information into cohesive ideas that will attract the interest of investors (sponsors) who provide the means to improve people's lives. The opportunity to work in this field may well be considered a great privilege—planting seeds . . . watching crops grow to maturity . . . and facilitating the actualization of dreams.

Grantsmanship includes the skill, practice, and art of obtaining grant funds from sponsors as well as the ethical management of awarded funds. It relates to any activity that moves an individual or a project team toward the submission of a fundable application, and, if successful in acquiring grant funding, toward the completion of activities to actualize the goals, objectives, outputs, and outcomes described in the proposal documents. Because this book focuses on the acquisition of funding (pre-award activities) rather than the execution of awarded proposals (post-award activities), the term "grant-seeking" will be used to represent primarily pre-award activities.

Grant-seeking processes include

- searching for grant opportunities;
- reading and evaluating sponsors' guidelines;
- learning about a sponsor's past award patterns and priorities;
- researching current best practices and knowledge in the discipline, topic, or activities of interest to the applicants that relate to a prospective project;
- facilitating collaborative relationships and exploring the combining of forces toward a creative project design;
- determining the needs and characteristics of those who will be served by a prospective project;
- developing project plans and budgets; and
- writing knowledgeably, convincingly, and with enthusiasm about the prospective project in all its parameters.

Grant-seeking is a genre all its own. Speaking broadly, the general population probably does not understand very much about how grant funds are acquired by organizations or individuals. Comparatively few have met a grant-writer, read or written an awarded proposal, served on a grants review panel, or executed the provisions outlined in an awarded grant proposal. In essence, the world of grantsmanship, especially in the humanities, is relatively obscure. Working in this realm might be analogous to working in a small foreign country. The residents of this land who have invested years of practice and dedication have acquired substantial skills and experiences to live relatively comfortably from the fruits of their efforts. It requires a specialized talent, but talent can be developed and achieved with practice—you need not be a genius or a prodigy. An investment of passionate interest plus ten thousand hours in the pursuit of any practice will yield mastery (Coyle, 2009)—but far less can make you very proficient.

On the other hand, those who only occasionally practice activities related to grant-seeking often struggle with the specialized language, the process, and the format. The ultimate challenge comes down to the dedication required to achieve an excellent product. Compound occasional grant-seeking efforts with the service-centered workload of a typical librarian, and you have ample cause for the general aversion to grant-seeking by many of those who work in libraries. And, nothing remains stagnant—sponsors change guidelines; methods for submitting proposals change with advances in technology; and more recently, some sponsors have sought to engage larger community involvement through social media–style application methods.

The education and development of a grant-seeker occurs slowly. Reading actually funded applications that have been awarded through a specific sponsor's grant program is by far the best teacher. And there is no substitute for learning how to prepare fundable grant proposals other than by submitting the best possible proposals over and over again. With practice you can develop competence and confidence—excellent foundations for building your capacity.

Initially a grant-seeker will not know what he or she is doing. Just like acquiring any new skill or developing an art form, you do the best you can with the knowledge and access to resources that you have. It would not be surprising that an applicant's first grant application submission does not get awarded. In many situations, however, there may be multiple opportunities to resubmit the same project proposal because many grant programs are offered on a recurring basis. At the next opportunity to prepare a proposal to the same sponsor, you can advance the proposal's qualities simply by improving over the initial submission. Time to reflect on reviewers' feedback, if this is available, will help to deepen your understanding of what it takes to succeed. By the third attempt, the grant-seeker has improved methods for communicating his or her intent and the story of a particular project. This is how grant-seeking skills can mature—like an onion, one skin at a time.

You should be cautious, however, of the shotgun approach to grant-seeking. There are those who prepare one version of a proposal and then submit this version to a variety of sponsors, with hopes that at least one sponsor will find it to be meritorious. This strategy is not recommended. There is a great risk that the sponsors will recognize your methodology and that your relationship with them will thereby be compromised. This is not to say that a proposal cannot be customized and tailored to meet the specific requirements of various sponsors.

Grant-Writing Differs from Other Styles of Writing

Grant-seeking calls for a particular style of writing not found in other disciplines. Academic writing, for example, is often an individual pursuit based on previous study of completed research. According to Rugg and Petre (2004), there are several different genres related to academic writing: tutorial papers, method-mongering papers, consciousness-raising papers, theoretical papers, review papers, demonstration of concept papers, and research methods papers. Generally the academic writer is principally answering a complex question, exposing an idea, or evaluating the ideas of others in a dispassionate manner (Porter, 2007). Further, the narrative "container" may have no prescribed word or page limit and typically employs a specialized language or jargon.

Grant-writing, by contrast, presents goals and objectives that a project team plans to achieve during a future period of time, to ultimately improve people's lives. It convincingly portrays the positive attributes of the applicant, its partners, and its staff members, with the goal of building confidence in the project idea, in the project's benefits, and in the competence of the designated team to deliver the proposed products and/or results. Of course, to achieve this end, a grant proposal must use language that will be accessible to any type of reviewer, regardless of the preparers' expertise in the field, the proposed problem to be solved, or the technology to be implemented. Because reviewers are commonly volunteers—colleagues like you who want to contribute their time and expertise to important causes—succinctness is often rewarded (Porter, 2007).

Next, consider the differences between grant-writing and fund-raising writing to support an organization's cause, program, or campaign. This mode of writing is used for donor communication, whether in a high-end ten-page brochure, in a letter, or in a wallet-sized card. Fund-raising documents often rely on a case statement—core information that justifies why funds are needed, and what the future donor's funds will achieve. Case statements answer questions such as:

- How does this organization serve people?
- Who is served by the organization?

- What vital services does the organization offer, and how does it deliver these services?
- What is the organization's track record, and future plans?
- How does the organization use the money it raises now, and what is its strategy for expending future funding?
- Why does the organization deserve a donor's support? (Foundation Center, 2015)

Donor acquisition writing differs from grant-writing in that its goal is to create interest in an organization, a cause, or a solution at a personal level. This type of "selling" often uses interpersonal language specifically tailored to individual donors being contacted. Fund-raising copy or media can be modified to be included in a grant proposal, but this content will only provide a fraction of the information required to complete a typical grant application package.

In contrast, the style of writing called for when requesting grant funding must be primarily responsive to a sponsor's guidelines, which provide specifications for the types of information required by reviewers, and which also matches with a sponsor's mission and priority interests. Sponsors' guidelines usually outline the requirements for eligible applicants, the maximum award amounts, the required start and end dates for grant periods, examples of fundable project types, and the allowable and disallowable expenses that sponsor funds can and cannot support.

The essential differences in these styles of writing can be analyzed by comparing their respective "containers." A grant proposal container is established by the sponsor's guidelines. Guidelines usually prescribe the type of content and information required and the order in which it should be presented. For an academic paper, the author has the freedom to select a format that is most beneficial in presenting his or her findings, analysis, or knowledge. The container for an academic paper may change because of the nature of its content, whereas the container for grant proposals changes as a result of a sponsor's requirements.

In terms of case statements, successful containers have been designed and tested by fund-raising professionals over many years. There are an infinite number of creative formats and formulas that will succeed in capturing a donor's heart and money depending on the type of fund-raising activity or cause being promoted. The container for materials designed for raising general operating funds, for instance, will be quite different from those wanting to generate capital campaign dollars. The text and the graphic presentation are designed to work together to quickly convince a prospective donor—who may be assumed to be a very busy person with lots of other interests—to make a contribution.

These three forms of containers differ greatly in communicating to their potential audiences. Each is "selling" an idea, analysis, or solution to a different audience. Academic papers are read by other academics, students, and researchers who are curious and knowledgeable about the specific topic being addressed. Donor solicitation letters or case statements are designed for prospective donors or general audiences. In the case of grant proposals, the audience is typically invisible, quite small, and unique for each grant opportunity. Grant reviewers generally remain invisible to applicants for many reasons, but primarily to support a system that protects their anonymity as they make decisions about award amounts and declinations.

"Selling" your project in grant proposals occurs through strategies employed to hook the reader into being interested in learning progressively more about the proposed project or request. Because the reviewers are likely not personally known to the applicant organization, the text is written in such a way as to convince them of the proposal's merits specifically in response to the sponsor's guidelines. Reviewers may be charged with reviewing hundreds of applications for a pool of dollars that likely can't support them all; so to be a contender a proposal must be, at a minimum, convincingly innovative, feasible, and reasonable in terms of the dollar amount requested.

Gray Is the Color of Grant-Seeking

Our culture provides "black-and-white" opportunities for those who complete tasks by precisely and successfully following detailed instructions. Following cooking recipes, completing online forms for preparing tax returns, or applying for a loan all have standardized procedures that support a successful outcome. By reading the "guidelines" and following the directions, your outcome quite often will be close to the desired result. If not, repeating the process with slight modifications based on additional information may get you there.

Conversely, grant-seekers work in an environment that is mostly "gray." Problems are likely to occur when grant-seekers assume that the process is always "black and white." The following examples illustrate some of the typical "gray" hues of grant-seeking norms:

1. Sponsor guidelines: These can vary widely. For long-standing program opportunities, the guidelines may be reliable and unchanging for many years. However, a new program may emerge that is designed hastily and promoted before its designers can realize the errors or contradicting information that they have included. For instance, the narrative instructions sometimes omit required content that is described in the criteria for evaluating the proposal. Or perhaps the guidelines— possibly written by an inexperienced staff member— fail to include instructions for describing the project or its significance.
2. Review process: It would be a mistake to believe that the review process for any grant program is black and white. An applicant should not assume that the sponsor has developed a logical review system, or has selected reviewers with sufficient experience or knowledge about the sponsor's programs or guidelines. Nor should you assume that criteria will be consistently or objectively applied during the review process. To mitigate this uncertainty, grant-seekers should attempt to learn as much as possible about how reviewers are selected and how future proposals will be reviewed. If the sponsor's program is new, there is a higher likelihood that kinks in its review system may impact a fair review of the proposals. Or, some reviewers will enter the process with a preconceived agenda to support certain types of proposals over others for a variety of reasons that may not coincide with review criteria. Manipulating the review process may not happen often, but when it does, it will likely be invisible to the applicants.
3. Sponsor solicited invitations: Not all funding opportunities are created equally or fairly. Consider the instance where a foundation's revenues are greater than expected during a given fiscal year and as a result, the foundation's grantmakers are unable to expend sufficient revenue during the year to avoid a tax penalty. These situations are sometimes resolved through direct solicitation of previously successful grantees by a sponsor's program officers. In these situations, a program officer will discuss the options through a one-on-one invitation with a respected potential applicant, arriving at a mutually agreed-upon fundable project and funding

amount. The invited applicant simply must submit the necessary documentation as instructed by the program officer to "fast-track" the award. An important lesson here is that cultivating good relationships with sponsor administrators can be a great advantage in your grant-seeking activities.

4. Deadlines: These are not always consistent among sponsors, although a fixed annual deadline is the norm. For some sponsors there may be a rolling deadline, meaning applications are welcome at any time and reviewed at scheduled review sessions throughout the year. Or there are no deadlines, and applicants can submit whenever they want with reviews taking place upon receipt of applications. In both of these cases, when the sponsor's budgets for awarded projects are exhausted, subsequent applicants are turned away or invited to submit early the next year.

Another issue related to fluctuations in deadlines can occur when a sponsor requires less than one year to complete a project. This can arise when sponsor #2 has secured "pass-through" funding from sponsor #1 for a particular funding program (e.g., National Network of Libraries of Medicine [NN/LM] receives funding from the National Institutes of Health [NIH]). It may be the case that NIH must expend the funds issued in January by a deadline in April. Consequently, when NN/LM promotes the call for proposals, its guidelines will stipulate that project funding must be expended and the project completed by April 30th.

The takeaway here is that as a grant-seeker, you will be in a constant learning mode—open to new information and experiences. The danger is to allow yourself to become complacent. Remaining curious about the parameters that each new sponsor and each new submission opportunity presents can lead to rewarding grant-seeking experiences.

It Is Not All About the Money

When the motivation for grant-seeking comes predominantly from a desire to increase an organization's budget or for fame and glory—and not for creating worthy projects that have the power to change people's lives—there can be an underlying risk to the project as a whole. It could be the case that a library's operating funds have been reduced and the library director believes that the difference can be made up in grant funding. Or in another example, an academic library's budget for acquisitions may have been reduced, or the library has lost funding for student workers. A library director might conclude that securing grant funding can be the solution to these deficits.

These scenarios offer an opportunity to discuss the roles that grant funding can play in a library. Grant funding rarely funds general operating expenses. Most grant funding received by academic and public libraries is project specific. To acquire grant funds that support a project that also provides a library with necessary support for its inherent needs requires not only grant-seeking strategies but also a best-match sponsor. Coming up with a project idea that has multiple benefits and beneficiaries can often include a strategy for meeting some of the library's needs, but it becomes possible only when the combined strategies support the project in a cohesive rather than contrived narrative.

Reviewers will be able to detect when a narrative and budget request resources that are not specific to actualizing a project, but rather include unnecessary costs for supporting existing permanent staff time, or acquiring permanent equipment. This approach is likely to seem disingenuous. If reviewers sense that the project, in actuality, is intended primarily to acquire external funding and secondarily to complete the project, then the proposal may be doomed.

The Stress and Unforeseen Benefits of Grant-Seeking

Grant deadlines will inevitably create stress, especially when the people involved work best under pressure—preferring to wait until the week prior to the deadline to get to work seriously. One of the major reasons people avoid participating in grant-seeking activities is no doubt because of the stress they create.

Another major stressor occurs when grant projects originate at the administrative level of a library and then are assigned to librarians to be developed and submitted. Damage to a culture of grantsmanship is likely to occur when a project team is charged to develop and submit a proposal by a library director or supervisor. If the project has nothing to do with the project team's aspirations, but instead only reflects the library administrator's interests, then one of the outcomes of the grant preparation process might well be resentment toward the project itself.

Grant projects that emerge naturally from within a library, through discovery, assessment, and creative thinking, by comparison, can contribute greatly to building enthusiasm for grant-seeking. From the point an individual has an "aha" moment, the project has the potential to attract others in the libraries and beyond, who can and want to contribute to the idea. There is no end to the possibilities when the momentum comes from a genuine desire to create something new, or repurpose something old.

This book presents strategies for supporting a culture of grantsmanship in libraries, the benefits of which can hardly be overstated. A culture by its nature involves deep collaboration. The potential joys and feelings of satisfaction produced by the journey of completing a fundable grant proposal, however, can be overshadowed by the stress of the looming deadline, or the prospect of a declination. But if an overarching goal of the project team, while developing the proposal, is to learn and to collaborate on an idea that has captured everyone's imagination, then the process is never for naught—regardless of the sponsor's final appraisal.

◎ Key Points

Librarians who want to acquire grant funding to actualize their project ideas benefit greatly from understanding the context in which this work is performed and rewarded.

- Funding to libraries was seminal to inspiring the creation of the United States as a country, and to developing the nonprofit sector.
- In recent years, libraries have suffered financial losses due to a variety of causes, especially the dependence on local tax revenue sources.
- Grantsmanship skills can be developed and honed through practice, reading proposals that have been awarded, and learning from grant reviewers' comments.
- Grant-writing is a unique style of writing that satisfies the requirements of reviewers based on the expectations of the sponsor from which an investment is being sought.
- Successful grant-seeking cannot consistently be achieved by simply following the sponsor's guidelines and submitting the required documentation.

- Don't let the stress of a deadline wipe out the other benefits of collaboratively creating a fundable proposal.

The next chapter describes strategies to identify potential partner organizations, and ways to combine forces with both partners and sponsors for proposing fundable and creative projects.

ⓖ References

Coffman, Steve. 2006. "Building a New Foundation: Library Funding." *Searcher* 14, no. 1 (January): 26. Academic Search Premier, EBSCO*host*.

Coyle, Daniel. 2009. *The Talent Code: Greatness Isn't Born. It's Grown. Here's How.* New York: Bantam Dell.

Foundation Center. 2015. "Knowledge Base: What Is a Case Statement? Where Can I Learn More about It?" Grant Space. September 15. http://grantspace.org/tools/knowledge-base/Funding-Research/Definitions-and-Clarification/case-statements.

Harvard University. 2015. "History of Harvard University." http://www.harvard.edu/history.

Jaeger, Paul T., Ursula Gorham, Lindsay C. Sarin, and John Carlo Bertot. 2013. "Libraries, Policy, and Politics in a Democracy: Four Historical Epochs." *Library Quarterly* 83, no. 2 (April): 168–69. http://www.jstor.org/stable/10.1086/669559.

Kelly, Michael. 2011. "Bottoming Out? Severe Cuts Today Put Big Question Marks on the Future." *Library Journal* 136, no. 1 (January): 28. Academic Search Premier, EBSCO*host*.

Library of Congress. 2006a. "Jefferson's Legacy: A Brief History of the Library of Congress." March 30. http://www.loc.gov/loc/legacy/loc.html.

———. 2006b. "On These Walls: Inscriptions and Quotations in the Buildings of the Library of Congress." January 11. http://www.loc.gov/loc/walls/madison.html.

———. 2015. "Web Guides: Primary Documents in American History: Morrill Act." July 15. http://www.loc.gov/rr/program/bib/ourdocs/Morrill.html.

Porter, Robert. 2007. "Why Academics Have a Hard Time Writing Good Grant Proposals." *Journal of Research Administration* 38, no. 2 (Fall): 37. ABI/INFORM Complete, ProQuest.

Rugg, Gordon, and Marian Petre. 2004. *The Unwritten Rules of PhD Research.* New York: Open University Press.

Schwartz, Meredith. 2013. "The Budget Balancing Act: Library Budgets Show Modest Improvement and Signs of More to Come." *Library Journal* 138, no. 1 (January): 38. Academic Search Premier, EBSCO*host*.

Weiner, Sharon G. 2005. "The History of Academic Libraries in the United States: A Review of the Literature." *Library Philosophy and Practice* 7, no. 2 (Spring): 2–3. http://digitalcommons.unl.edu/libphilprac/58.

CHAPTER 2

Collaborative Concepts and Practical Approaches

GRANT-SEEKING ACTIVITIES NATURALLY stimulate an environment of partnership and creativity. This chapter discusses the basic principles and suggested approaches of how each of these phenomena can evolve prior to and during the proposal development process.

Basics of Grant-Seeking with Partners

There are a variety of funding programs and categories for which library grant support is available. These include support for facilities, outreach, training, preservation, research, digitization, cataloging, and even support for fund-raising, as well as many other types of endeavors. Now, due to the prevalence of electronic application submission, in general the competition for grant resources has increased dramatically. To assertively compete in this new arena, applicants increasingly opt to boost their chances by inviting others to play in their collective project sandbox. The synergy of working together can often yield results that go far beyond what an individual effort can produce.

Project proposals featuring active collaborative participation, especially from outside the applicant's organization, generally are stronger and more fundable proposals. Combining forces across disciplines, departments, and organizations generates increased creative thinking and leverages a potential project's resources, which can contribute a great deal to help a grant application stand out from the pack. If you could walk briefly in the sponsor's shoes you would readily see that funding a project that includes three active and different organizations allows the sponsor to support three applicants rather than one.

Beyond this, there can be strength in numbers. The biggest risk for a sponsor may be supporting a project that is singularly dependent on one or two key people from one organization. Circumstances can change once a project has been awarded. People might leave their jobs, move, get sick, or have babies; many situations can cause key people to be unable to participate in the completion of a grant project. Invariably, having broad commitment and involvement will add value, and possibly a bit more security to the sponsor's award investment.

Ways to Combine Forces

In the early 1990s, partnerships and collaborative activities were beginning to flourish in the nonprofit sector. Researchers for the Wilder Foundation set out to examine this trend. Analyzing their findings, the researchers concluded that organization staff and volunteers work with each other and with external entities generally in three major modalities: they cooperate, they coordinate, and they collaborate (Winer and Ray, 1996). Another significant modality in which people also have opportunities to combine forces is through mentoring relationships.

The Wilder Foundation researchers further defined these three modes of working with others in order to help the field distinguish the characteristics of each mode. Moving from cooperating to coordinating, and finally to collaborating is a progression involving increases in the level of effort, interdependence, and risk among those individuals and organizations seeking to work with each other.

Beginning with cooperation, the researchers surmised that this modality was the simplest and least intrusive. It involves no risk for either party but requires some minimal level of communication. During cooperative activities, both of the participating individuals or entities retain their separateness in the use of their own resources, and in resulting benefits received from the cooperative effort.

Cooperative activities are ubiquitous in the library world largely because of the existence of the library as a public place. The use of library space by outside organization representatives, for instance, to distribute promotional materials for an educational event being presented at another venue, or to recruit volunteers for a project, or to solicit signatures for a petition could be considered to be cooperative. In these cases the library benefits from informing their patrons or allowing patrons to choose to participate in something new; and the organization promoting the event, seeking volunteers or signatures, also benefits from having access to a facility and its patrons. This is a very passive, informal way to share resources.

The second mode in which organizations work together is to coordinate. Coordinating with external organizations requires more communication, planning, and effort among participating entities, and can pose greater risks. Again, libraries have long traditions of coordinating activities with outside entities such as offering services, events, educational programs, exhibits, and outreach. In these examples, available resources likely are more abundant and benefits tend to be more mutually recognized.

Collaboration is the third and most challenging way in which organizations and individuals combine forces, possibly because of the many risks these types of projects and programs usually present. This type of working relationship is distinguishable based on the activities that require extensive planning and defined communication roles and channels, and contributions of resources from both entities that are usually combined and shared in new ways. The commitment to work in this new structure usually comes from a common mission or purpose to solve a problem, fill a gap, or to take advantage of the leveraging of extant resources to create something new and valuable.

Examples of collaboration abound in libraries, both out of need and out of opportunity. Consortial relationships to stretch limited resources and add purchasing power are good examples of collaboration. Consider the many hours of work that it takes to communicate, plan, negotiate, and recruit participant libraries when one of these consortia is in the development stages.

Another common example of collaboration can be found in planning and executing digitization projects. In these instances, several organizations combine forces to convert similarly themed materials to digital format so as to provide broad access to these materials through a common online portal. Over time, these types of collaborations have become more commonplace, largely through the provision of grant funding. And because there have been so many different digital initiatives created to share a wide variety of materials online, the know-how for achieving success has been tried and tested repeatedly, allowing for the transference of this knowledge to others wanting to join the effort.

Finally, beyond the three modes of working together identified by the Wilder Foundation, the mentoring of one organization by staff members of an outside entity is the fourth way in which organizations can combine forces. This often occurs in collaborative environments where those in one organization have indispensable expertise to contribute to a project that the collaborating organization lacks.

For instance, when libraries, historical organizations, archives, or museums join up to combine collections for wider public findability and accessibility through a single digital portal, these representative groups usually follow the lead of the most experienced staff members. Often the library that hosts advanced digital collections has the capacity to mentor and lead less experienced collaborators in all the various digitization requirements and standards to complete such projects. And in the pursuit of grant funds, a library with advanced digital collections likely employs staff members with extensive grant-seeking experience as well. In these cases, the mentoring library's key personnel involved in such a project can play a valuable leadership and educational role in constructing the actual project parameters, methods, and standards.

Virtually any grant proposal will benefit from including one or more of these modalities, and vividly describing how the participating library plans to combine forces with other outside partners. Further, using these types of precise terms—cooperation, coordination, collaboration, and mentorship—to describe the relationship of partnering libraries or community organizations can elevate the quality of the grant application presentation.

In grant application narratives, the term "collaboration" has become overly used to describe activities that are not necessarily collaborative. The term has been misused to describe a relationship between two organizations that may actually be cooperative or coordinative. These more passive and less risk-laden modes of combining forces do not typically receive as high marks from grant reviewers as those that employ mentorship or true collaboration plans and activities.

Finding Potential Partners and Discovering Hidden Assets

When it comes to successful grant-seeking, scanning your environment for potential partners never stops. Librarians are perfectly skilled in this regard—to identify and assess future partners by searching for information about other potentially strong partnering organizations. Another essential skill commonly found among librarians is the ability to converse with "strangers." With these two strengths in hand, library employees can expect to do very well when it comes to building grant projects that combine forces with qualified project contributors.

Searching for potential partners begins with the understanding that what you are seeking to learn about is another organization's assets and how and why these assets relate to supporting your proposed project's aspirations. "Assets" in this context refers to all the available resources within an organization. For libraries, the list of assets can be long and varied, including: space; collections; staff skill sets, time, and networks; computer systems and software; community support, volunteers, and funding.

The idea of mapping multiple organizations' and individuals' assets as a means for leveraging partnerships to serve the greater good of a community was developed by the team of John P. Kretzmann and John L. McKnight, faculty members at Northwestern University in the Center for Urban Affairs and Policy Research. Their studies of how to develop and sustain community resiliency led to the concept of asset mapping, described in their published guide, *Building Communities from the Inside Out*, which focuses on identifying readily available tangible and intangible community assets. These assets may be hidden, but once identified can be rallied to strengthen a community, regardless of its economic condition. Interviewing those in a community, in outside organizations, or in other libraries is one way to find hidden assets (Kretzmann and McKnight, 1993).

The irony is that many who work in libraries or other organizations are unaware of their own entity's assets. This is largely because taking time out from daily responsibilities to learn about what others do well, what they are passionate about, or what they know about is not necessarily considered to be a valued activity. Learning about all your library's assets, first through conversations and later through reading employee résumés and published articles by colleagues and sharing conference presentations, is an avenue that will contribute to creating a library's asset map—whether it resides on a spreadsheet or in your mind.

Next, read the newspaper and listen to your local public radio station. These sources will reveal possible assets and local organizations for contributing to your project. Reading journal articles, or library industry publications produced by the Association of College and Research Libraries or the American Library Association, or attending conference presentations related to the topic of the project at hand can uncover relevant national assets. Continuous learning about the strengths and interests of others, and their resources, may be the most effective way to identify those who will be the best potential supporters of your proposed grant project.

Another way to tap into potential partners is to present a large-group facilitated process that provides opportunities for convening potential partners, known as the World Café. This methodology was created by Juanita Brown, PhD, and David Isaacs as a means for hosting "conversations that matter" for solving community issues, creating a new program, or contributing in other ways to improve organizations and communities. Through short, focused conversations (twenty to thirty minutes each) with three to five invited guests at each table, the process methodology is to elicit answers to a single question or a few related questions at a time. The guests then rotate to other tables to learn of other discussions related to the same question(s), and to form deeper answers through several rounds of conversations, each time with new people (Brown, 2002). Strangers in this type of environment can walk away with new relationships and networks, new knowledge, and possible future project partners.

The staff at the Museum of Science and Industry (MOSI) in Tampa has used this method for years and has established itself as an expert community collaborator. For instance, MOSI "hosted a 400 person World Café with members of the Giant Screen Theatre Association, and another with the international board of the Association of Science and Technology Centers. In both cases, World Café conversations helped identify and prioritize key issues and what actionable steps we're going to take to address those issues" (Brown, 2005: 30). You can imagine all the potential partners and new expert collegial relationships MOSI staff members were able to walk away with.

Collaborating with Strangers (CoLAB) workshops is another facilitated process available for finding potential project partners. These workshops are based on principles highlighted in the CoLAB Planning Series developed by the author in 2002 for quickly revealing untapped assets. Currently presented at the University of Florida, University of Washington, and University of North Texas Libraries,

> CoLABs connect "strangers" and/or colleagues to hidden commonalities, expertise, resources, networks and creative opportunities. The CoLAB Planning Series® is a set of group facilitative processes (16 to 120 individuals) which supports one-on-one "speed meetings" where participants quickly reveal their passions, skills and resources that may otherwise take months of conversations to uncover. Along with providing information on the basics of collaboration and methods for developing creativity, CoLAB's specific purpose is to facilitate the 1) discovery of hidden resources and/or potential collaborative relationships; 2) generation of new ideas for innovation and research; and, 3) problem solving of issues by leveraging extant yet untapped assets. . . . One of the primary ways in which CoLABs have benefited individuals and communities is in creating safe and engaging "café" environments in which participants from various fields (or organizations) can meet each other, exchange information and ideas and, together, build new foundations to start or create projects. (de Farber, 2013: 1–2)

Using asset-based community development methods such as these allows a project team to focus on opportunities for leveraging what is available and accessible as a means of improving a situation, resolving a need, and successfully implementing a solution. This method also is known as capacity-focused development (Kretzmann and McKnight, 1993). This can be compared to needs-based project design approaches where the needs of a community or organization are emphasized and resources for meeting those needs or solving a problem are not readily known or available. In the needs-based model, securing external funding, or resources, as opposed to leveraging a community's extant assets, is commonly seen as the means to achieve the solution. Consequently, "this approach takes longer to measure progress, doesn't necessarily broaden participation, and often fosters a sense of pessimism—because plans are difficult to execute and require external resources. Need-based planning frequently leads to the questioning of a project's feasibility" (de Farber, 2014: 2). This type of approach also can take longer to complete and may result in less community buy-in.

Convening Potential Partners

Once assets and their owners have been identified, conversations that explore possibilities of participation and commitment should occur next. This activity may read easier on the page than it plays out in reality. Inviting and facilitating potential players to the project development and negotiation table poses several challenges to both experienced and novice grant project teams during the preparation process.

First, choosing those to invite to the table requires planning. If the deadline is imminent, then selecting potential partnering libraries with librarians and library employees who have previous successful experiences participating in grant-funded projects will be most helpful. Additionally, recruiting an excess of potential partners for the project will provide the team with options in the event that some will decline the opportunity to participate.

At this point, the team should be prepared to deliver the first communication inviting organizations to the table. This e-mail should contain:

1. A working project title
2. A brief description or abstract of the project including its objectives and deliverables
3. The proposed role to be played by the prospective partner
4. Planned benefits for the prospective partner
5. The deadline by which a response is needed

The issue of whether funds will be available to support activities performed by the potential partner, or whether contributed in-kind resources are needed from the potential partner, should be discussed during the first meeting, regardless of whether the meeting takes place in person, by phone, or virtually. This means that it will be necessary to have a draft budget and draft timeline (even if these are very preliminary) in hand prior to making the invitation. People who are collaborating with "strangers" for the first time find it easier to respond to existing ideas and plans rather than starting from scratch. If the library's project team has not developed these two documents, then inviting others to join the project may be premature.

In the process of cultivating potential grant project partners, confidence generates trust. Before you invite another entity to join the grant project, you should be able to clearly articulate the potential benefits—including possible funding—they might derive from their involvement. For the project team, this can make the difference between getting to the finish line with a fundable proposal, or missing the deadline because there wasn't enough time to flesh out the budget. Partners or collaborators are always going to be interested in "what's in it for me?" Having the answer to this question at the outset when courting a potential grant project "marriage" will expedite the decision making that must occur among partner organization administrators.

Not all projects will yield funding for participating partners. Sometimes the benefits will include greater exposure of a hidden collection, new resources for educating patrons, or research results that will guide the future of library professionals. Often these benefits are sufficient to engage the commitment of external partners.

Because of the sensitive nature of these initial discussions, it might be best to secure the assistance of an experienced facilitator who can serve as a neutral player in guiding the conversation. If this is an option, the librarian leading the project may adopt the role of project expert, answering questions directly related to the project, but allowing the facilitator to manage the conversation about prospective funding availability for the partners, if any is planned, or required documentation and deadlines that may need to be met.

Partnering with a Sponsor

Once the project team has identified its partners, although some may be only tentatively committed to the project, initial contact should be made with the selected sponsor's program staff. Contacting a sponsor's program officer early in the process of preparing a proposal will yield the most benefits. The goal is to establish a cooperative mentoring relationship. Much of the same information sent to prospective partners can be repurposed to introduce the proposed project to the sponsor's program officer.

What is important to remember is that collaborative grant-seeking includes viewing the sponsor as both a customer and a mentor. Sponsoring agencies prefer to receive competitive and eligible grant applications; the more competitive the applications, the closer a sponsor can move toward achieving its mission and vision. Often, this preference only can be realized when the sponsor's staff members can interact directly with applicants, coaching them to submit a strong application. Seeking direct input on the quality of a project team's proposal ideas, content, budget, and recommendations for selecting authors to prepare letters of commitment or support, for example, can lead to better results. Approaching the sponsor's representatives with a cooperative and mentee attitude creates a supportive, mutually beneficial, and satisfying relationship.

It appears, for whatever reason, that grant applicants often seem reluctant to make contact with sponsor agency employees for guidance and advice. These employees are working to achieve excellence in the field of philanthropy and, particularly for governmental sponsors, they are typically willing to offer constructive feedback. There is always a chance, of course, that a program officer will discourage an idea or a strategy. But it would be best to determine this early in the process so that adjustments can be made or proposals can be delayed if they require an entirely new strategy.

Finally, it is important to sincerely and formally thank those in sponsoring agencies for any assistance they provide along the way. This step should occur after the submission of the complete proposal and prior to the receipt of award or declination notification results.

⑥ Dynamics of Partner Connections

Challenges of Partnering with "Strangers"

Most people would prefer to work with others they know and trust. Unfortunately, when creating a fundable grant proposal, this is not always possible, especially if the sponsor prefers or requires that applicants include committed representation by external partnering organizations as official members of the project team. When strangers get together physically or virtually to create a grant proposal package, there can be lots of surprises. These initial collaborative relationships should be considered to be "short-term or itinerant" in nature—they exist to accomplish a specific task and likely will not be reconstituted unless the grant is awarded (Rubin, 1998). Assuming that everything will go smoothly—because you believe everyone's intentions are good and all members of the project team are enthusiastic about the idea—can lead to disappointments. When people first interact with each other, they begin to sense differences in personalities and working styles among the members. To accommodate these differences, the project leader or facilitator will need to ensure that frequent two-way inquiry and communication is achieved.

Hank Rubin, PhD, in his book *Collaboration Skills for Educators and Nonprofit Leaders*, describes some of the disruptive personality types that may show up in collaborative endeavors. These include a variety of saboteurs you should be cautious of:

- The "Malicious Saboteur," who seeks to undermine the endeavor because of past resentments directed at a project team member.
- The "Limelight Saboteur," whose ego must be stroked or validated often.
- The "Power Grabbing Saboteur," who regardless of the situation or expertise, must perform the decision-maker role.
- The "Lone Wolf Saboteur," who may be an active and equal participant in decision making but doesn't bring anything to the table in the form of resources.
- The "Ambivalent Saboteur," who may send various representatives to participate on the project team due to a lack of commitment.
- The "Sloppy Thinking or Distracted Saboteur," who lacks the ability to focus on the project at hand, and steers discussions that become redundant, confusing, and regressive.

Rubin's words of encouragement, when it comes to managing "saboteurs," point to the existing strengths of a project team's members: "(1) . . . an earnest belief that they have a stake in the success of the collaboration . . . and (2) . . . an environment . . . that both enables and expects direct and honest communication between partners, then other leaders among our collaborative partners will be motivated to help us confront and manage the saboteurs" (Rubin, 1998: 78).

Protocols for Supporting Partnerships

Once the partners have been secured, the librarian leading the effort to prepare the proposal package should be aware of some of the basic methods and requirements for creating a positive working environment. The following list of documents, prepared in advance of convening the project team with its outside partners, can ensure a solid beginning to discussions, plans, and negotiations:

1. Guidelines for the specific grant opportunity
2. Customized checklist that interprets the required proposal elements and review criteria (see chapter 5 for details)
3. Template of the letter of commitment that confirms each partner's involvement and designated role (see chapter 6 for details)
4. A draft budget that proposes expenses needed for the project, even if this is in the very early stages of development (see chapter 6 for details)
5. A draft timeline that proposes when activities will take place, even if this is just a guess (see chapter 6 for details)

The first meeting agenda likely will take at least an hour and a half to two hours, depending on the number of participants. Table 2.1 shows an agenda example.

Table 2.1. Example Agenda for the First Project Partners Meeting

SUGGESTED TIME FRAME	ACTION ITEM
5 minutes/person	Share self-introductions including what role(s) each participant is willing to play based on the initial discussion, and why each wants to participate (what's in it for me?).
15 minutes	Determine how documents will be shared (Google Docs, wiki, Dropbox, etc.), who will perform the final copyediting, and who will be responsible for completing the final packaging and submission.
30 minutes	Determine who will be the applicant organization, the project director and codirectors, and the key personnel to be described in the proposal (those who have required expertise to ensure the project is completed successfully).
30–45 minutes	Review and discuss each element of the checklist, especially the criteria; this may also include discussion of content to be emphasized such as unique assets, or the timing of the project vis-à-vis other positive coinciding supportive activities.
30 minutes or more for this planning process	Discuss and make decisions about who will contribute which sections of the narrative and attachments, with an estimation of the timing for when the first round of drafts for each element will be shared with the team. The applicant institution usually prepares the Excel budget drafts and final budget forms, including a compilation of detail expenses and in-kind contributions provided by individual partner organizations.
10 minutes	Determine who will take and distribute notes for the project team at each meeting. Schedule the next meeting(s).

By preparing for and completing the first meeting in such a thorough and organized manner, the effect will be to demonstrate confidence and mutual respect for the time being invested in the project, as a means for developing trust among the partners. If this can be achieved early on and then maintained throughout, the proposal development process will have a good chance of being predictably secure, especially under the stress generated by the grant submission deadline.

Other factors that may impact the stress of project team members occur when some members are located off-site—whether in a local community or in a campus unit away from the library—which makes them invisible. Working in a virtual environment means that communication about editing and information gathering must be shared openly and frequently so as to avoid wasted time by project team members who only can assume what others are doing because they work remotely. Also, ensuring that only one person at a time is making edits to a working document can contribute to a less confusing production process. Project team members also can support the development process by including, while they edit, comments related to the reasons for their proposed major edits and changes. This allows the project leader the opportunity to accept or decline the changes without necessarily having to contact each editor to understand the rationale for each change.

Partnerships That Inspire Creativity

Sponsors look for applications that propose innovative ways of achieving a desired result, with the ultimate goal of improving people's lives. Because partnerships bring together a variety of organizations, individuals, and assets that may never have collaborated in the past, the opportunities for generating creative methodologies or end results can be abundant. And, if the organizations are dissimilar to one another, then these partnerships may have the greatest potential for invention.

Libraries, especially, present such a variety of disciplines from which creativity can emerge. Because of these diverse assets, it would be difficult to find a topic that would be outside a library's scope. For instance, combining the skills of a playwright with a library's collection that contains original first-person accounts of a historic event could result in a theatre production that exposes a collection's hidden stories, promotes the importance of preserving family documents, or popularizes research into a previously hidden collection. Such a project could contribute to an entirely new genre of theatre. (Learn more about this project in chapter 3.)

Infusing artistic assets into a project is one way of encouraging creativity, but not the only way. How about combining tourism development activities and libraries? A library's assets may include historical maps or architectural documents related to a community that when digitized and featured in digital maps, along with stories from historians and archivists, could create a mobile web application for use by tourists. (More information about this project is available in chapter 3.)

When it comes to social work or legal services, public libraries are increasingly coconvening and partnering with social workers and attorneys, many of whom are delivering professional services in the library. And librarians are making rounds with medical students, developing consumer health libraries in hospitals, and training health care workers about where to find reliable digital resources for their patients.

Combining multiple types of assets into cohesive projects or programs can inspire grantmakers and donors to take notice of the possibilities library employees have potential to create. Submitting grant proposals to sponsors, beyond requesting funding support, serves the purpose of informing others of the powerful, creative work happening in libraries. When these projects receive grant awards, they become excellent vehicles for broadly promoting the library sector's good work.

Key Points

Combining forces with partners has become a standard practice in grant-seeking, and increasingly is required by sponsors. When working with external library partners, it is important to keep these points in mind:

- The four ways of working with partnering entities include cooperating, coordinating, collaborating, and mentoring.
- Describing, in specific terms, the ways in which a library is actively partnering with other entities can build a sponsor's trust that sufficient project planning has occurred.
- Learning about potential community "assets" and future partners is a continuous process for grant-seekers.

- Early in the planning process, participating partner representatives should have the opportunity to disclose their organization's motivation for joining the grant project team, and to share what their organization expects to receive—including funding if this is necessary—to reduce future confusion and conflicts when finalizing budgets.
- Librarians should always take advantage of opportunities to partner with a sponsor to improve a project idea or any element of an application submission.
- At the initial meeting for convening partners, the project team goal is to create confidence in the capacity of the team to complete and submit a fundable proposal.
- Creativity is often generated by projects that combine forces with a variety of different disciplines and expertise.

The next chapter presents the details of each step for creating a grant-seeking program within a library.

References

Brown, Juanita. 2002. *The World Café: A Resource Guide for Hosting Conversations That Matter*. Mill Valley, CA: Whole Systems Associates.

———. 2005. *The World Café: Shaping Our Futures through Conversations That Matter*. San Francisco: Berrett-Koehler.

de Farber, Bess. 2013. "Initial Steps to Create the CoLAB Planning Series® Workshops Designed to Spark Collaborations and Creativity through Revealing and Leveraging Community Assets." The Institutional Repository at the University of Florida. December 13. http://ufdc.ufl.edu/IR00003505/00002.

———. 2014. "Conditions and Guiding Principles: How to Produce Beneficial CoLAB Planning Series® Workshop Results." The Institutional Repository at the University of Florida. September 19. http://ufdc.ufl.edu/IR00003847/00002.

Kretzmann, John P., and John L. McKnight. 1993. *Building Communities from the Inside Out: A Path toward Finding and Mobilizing a Community's Assets*. Evanston, IL: John Kretzmann and John McKnight.

Rubin, Hank. 1998. *Collaboration Skills for Educators and Nonprofit Leaders*. Chicago: Lyceum Books.

Winer, Michael, and Karen Ray. 1996. *Collaboration Handbook: Creating, Sustaining, and Enjoying the Journey*. Saint Paul, MN: Amherst H. Wilder Foundation.

CHAPTER 3

Creating a Library Grant-Seeking Program

THIS CHAPTER OUTLINES STEP-BY-STEP processes for establishing an internal "mini-grant" program that will offer practical grant-writing experiences while cultivating a collaborative grantsmanship culture in libraries. A cultural environment within a library system that encourages and inspires grant-seeking efforts can yield high returns, not only in terms of financial rewards but more fundamentally in terms of nurturing the creative ideas of staff and motivating imaginative activity. A powerful boost toward developing this kind of culture can be achieved by establishing a competitive internal grantmaking program. While internally funded awards stimulate collaborative and innovative projects in an infinite number of ways, they also make huge contributions to convening project teams with representative membership from throughout a library in unique configurations. When these teams are supported by operational systems—human resources, facilities, fiscal services, and so forth—these systems also will contribute to an environment conducive to grant-seeking. Such a program can be initiated and supported by a small pot of internal funds.

The benefits of an internal program extend in many directions. A primary benefit is the learning opportunity provided for inexperienced grant-seekers. This learning process is incentivized by the opportunity for librarians to access financial awards for projects of their own creation within a program that offers a safe and friendly starting point for first-time applicants. An internal program also provides a means for experienced grant-writers to advance projects they care about, access project funds, and ultimately to practice their grantsmanship skills. As librarians learn to create fundable projects, they are also learning the grants preparation process by constructing a proposal from the inception of an idea through to submission of a complete proposal. The more positive experiences librarians and staff have in developing and executing grant-funded projects, the more a library's culture of grantsmanship will grow, thus making the activities required to be successful in performing grants-related work more commonplace in the library world. The major steps for establishing such a program are:

- Step 1. Allocate a funding source and annual granting budget amount.
- Step 2. Establish a grants committee.
- Step 3. Create the application guidelines.
- Step 4. Coach applicants and project team to prepare fundable applications.
- Step 5. Conduct the application review process.
- Step 6. Support awarded teams to achieve successful project completion.

Creating an Internal Library Grantmaking Program

If librarians and library administrators want to build a grant-seeking program, then establishing an internally funded mini-grant program is an excellent option for achieving this aim. Among other benefits, it will encourage and inspire librarians and other library staff to learn about grantsmanship activities using practical, hands-on approaches rather than relying on theoretical classroom training. In addition, libraries can strengthen future grant-seeking activities through mini-grant procedures that mirror, as closely as possible, the experience of planning, writing, and submitting a complete grant application to an external sponsor. This process will produce the most successful and desirable results when administered in a supportive learning environment.

Step 1: Find a Funding Source and Allocate a Grantmaking Budget

To start a mini-grant program, funds must be allocated to cover the expenses outlined in the awarded mini-grant budgets. An investment of between $500 and $5,000 is sufficient to initiate an annual program. Larger libraries may have the means to allocate as much as $25,000 to $50,000 or more per year for these endeavors, thus supporting the possibility of two funding cycles. Funds received annually from a corporate sponsor, or from used-book sales or other fund-raising activities, also can be excellent sources for supporting mini-grants. The goal here is to designate a permanent fund within a library's annual budget for the internal grantmaking program. When a library's administrators are able to make this long-term commitment, they essentially commit to establishing a grant-seeking program and growing a culture of grantsmanship within their library.

With an emphasis on grant-seeking, it should be widely known among a library's personnel that the primary purpose of funds dedicated to a mini-grant program is not necessarily to fund creative or needed library projects; rather, it should be made clear that the main purpose is to develop knowledge, skills, and interests in pursuing grant-related experiences. Benefits of the grant projects themselves are a significant incidental benefit of establishing this type of small internal grantmaking program.

There are certainly many academic and public libraries that offer librarians and staff a variety of opportunities to submit proposals for small internal grant awards or budget allocations to offset expenses related to special projects. The purpose of these opportunities is often to disburse such funds for meritorious purposes that move a library's strategic priorities forward, that spark innovation, or to meet important needs that can't be funded otherwise.

For instance, the University of Houston Libraries supports such initiatives through a Strategic Directions Microgrant Program (SDMP) inaugurated in 2007, which focuses on "expanding the Libraries' virtual presence; becoming an integrated teaching and learning center; enriching support for scholarly communication; and, rebranding the Libraries." These "strategic directions" are intended to move the UH Libraries' activities closer to those ends, while using formal application mechanisms, to foster an "entrepreneurial spirit" (Getz, Bennett, and Linden, 2014: 56–58).

At the University of Iowa (UI) Libraries, any employee is eligible to submit an application. Funding at UI Libraries is intended to support creative and innovative experiments. Documentation about this internal grant process, provided by the assistant to the university librarian at UI, Kelly Avant, indicates that eligible projects can expand or make a current service more efficient, initiate a new service, or make current resources stronger. Funding for the program comes from the Library Innovation, Service, and Entrepreneurship fund—an endowment UI Libraries typically receives five applications and funds two from $400 to $5,000 each year.

The University of California, Irvine (UCI), Libraries has offered the Innovation Grant Program since 2012. Some examples of projects resulting from $500 to $10,000 awards include "Video Game Lab Pilot Project"; "Online Archive of UCI History"; and "AnteaterTag@UCI: Metadata Games Pilot Project." Internal documentation received from the assistant university librarian for administrative services at UCI, Kevin Ruminson, indicates that participation in these grant-seeking endeavors, beyond stimulating these creative projects, has contributed to developing a culture of proposal development. Efforts to execute this secondary goal include supporting activities to find appropriate funding opportunities beyond this Innovation Grant Program. This program's guidelines share some preferred characteristics of prospective proposals that include qualities such as demonstrating excellence, or uniqueness; or proposals that address campus priorities, produce outcomes that improve efficiencies or effectiveness, or have been unsuccessful in attracting support from external sponsors.

The Seattle Public Library provides its library system employees with opportunities to apply for funds using online forms outlining community needs, opportunities, and benefits. A form along with guidelines provided by the library's community partnerships and government relations staff member, Chance Hunt, requests details about physical space requirements and necessary staffing support for presenting innovative programs. The applications are first approved by managers and then reviewed by the Programming Committee. Awards have ranged from a few hundred dollars to over $2,500 for projects such as "Seattle Writes: NaNoWriMo," "Lego Mania!," and the "Chinese Family Finance Workshop Series."

These excellent examples provide ways to design an internal small grants program. Converting an existing library grantmaking program into one that also provides training and mentoring in proposal writing, however, can result in an array of added professional development benefits. Participants will have opportunities to gain valuable skills and experiences as proposal writers, project planners, project directors, or team members to prepare them for their future service on externally sponsored grant project teams.

Step 2: Establish a Grants Committee

To administer the mini-grant program, invite a small group of librarians and library staff (from three to eleven members, depending on the size of the library) who have the most experience in project planning/management, preparing grant documentation, and assessing processes. This group can be called the grants committee or the grants management/review committee. Qualified participants might include those with obvious successful grant-writing experiences as well as those with accounting, proposal writing (not necessarily for grants, but for business or other types of planning documentation), and marketing and promotion experience. Valuable skills possessed by library personnel who specialize in other types of library operations can be helpful in assessing the merits of submitted mini-grant proposals. Areas of specialization might include acquisitions; information, reference, and referral; community development, education, special collections, and digital media; or any of the various disciplines found in libraries.

Two prerequisites to participation should be that a grants committee member be genuinely interested in serving for one to three years and be an enthusiastic supporter of efforts to assist librarians and other library staff in grant-seeking activities and protocols—with the ultimate goal of expanding the number of fundable proposals being submitted to external sponsors. Lacking this commitment and enthusiasm among committee members, a competitive grantmaking program can quickly devolve into a forum for negativity, thus subverting the committee's mission of stimulating a supportive climate and readiness for grant-seeking. Staggering the terms of service for grants committee members can result in effective mentoring of new members and in perpetuating institutional memory. Transferring cumulated information, including historical protocols and past committee decisions and experiences, to new members can significantly enrich the context of their service and guide their decisions on the committee. This can be a very important element in helping to sustain high standards for a mini-grants program.

Step 3: Create the Application Guidelines

The grants committee will develop guidelines for submission of mini-grant proposals. There are several important questions to consider when developing the guidelines:

- Who will be eligible to apply?
- What type of projects will be considered "fundable" or appropriate?
- What will be the maximum award?
- How many applications can an individual submit?
- What will be the annual deadline(s) and grant period(s) for application submissions?
- How will applications be evaluated?
- How can the application guidelines frame a mini-grant program that rewards projects for including collaborative partners?
- How does the committee deal with "conflicts of interest" during the review process?
- What information should mini-grant applications contain?

Who Will Be Eligible to Apply?

When programs are being initiated, it may be best to encourage anyone in the library system to apply. Ideally, making the mini-grant program open to any librarian and possibly to any permanent library staff applicant can demonstrate that the intent of the program is to encourage and increase grant-writing activities in general, regardless of the level of experience of the applicant or his or her employment status within the library. There may be some employees who have had past successful experiences in the grants world—either as project directors, project team members, or as administrators—who understand, for instance, project planning, design, or budgeting. The more people who are welcomed by the opportunity to apply, the more applications will be generated and the more practice and learning will take place. Because grant project planning may involve the cooperation of staff from any library department, allowing any library employee to apply for a mini-grant may stimulate practical grant preparation experiences without restricting participation.

The grants committee may be tempted to consider limiting the pool of mini-grant applicants only to first-time library grant-writers/project directors. Members of a committee, especially those working in large libraries with a large pool of potential applicants or very small libraries with limited grantmaking funds, may be inclined to adopt this approach simply to reduce the number of potential applicants. Limiting opportunities for participation, however, may produce the undesirable consequence of stifling the potential enthusiasm within the library for supporting a new program. On the other hand, a significant advantage of including more experienced grant-seekers in the program is that these librarians will help raise the standard of proposal writing through their participation. These applications may serve as initial models for others to emulate (for instance, in terms of quality of content or style, or innovativeness). Another undesirable consequence of limiting these applications to first-time grant-seekers could be that experienced applicants might opt to create a proposal and then convince a first-time applicant to serve as the "project director" and official applicant, thus trying to beat the system.

What Type of Projects Will Be Considered "Fundable" or Appropriate?

The committee has the option of proposing either a narrow or a broad focus for eligible internal grant projects. They may choose to limit the scope of eligible projects because the library has particular needs, say, for community outreach projects or acquisition of resources within a specific collection or strategic goals to develop a more robust digital library. All of these foci may be worthy of support. Rather than restricting types of fundable projects to specific themes, a grants committee that embraces the goal of expanding the library's culture of grantsmanship can take the long view that fostering innovative and collaborative projects, without restriction, will ultimately achieve that goal by using a more inclusive strategy. Furthermore, increasing the capacity of librarians to develop both feasible and innovative projects, regardless of the project, then creates the expanded potential for increasing externally sponsored grant awards, which ubiquitously include "innovation" and "collaboration" as major criteria for evaluating the quality of proposals.

What Will Be the Maximum Award?

Several considerations come into play when determining the answer to this question. For instance, if a library's available funding for mini-grant projects is $500 per year, then the committee might decide the maximum award can be $125 per application, which will produce at least four awards annually. If the library has fewer than ten librarians and staff, $500 can be enough to get started. It only takes a little imagination to envision what a librarian might do with this small amount of money. Hosting collaborative planning meetings and including lunch, or providing refreshments during an outreach event; funding travel for a site visit to learn about other library programs; purchasing supplies or swag; covering printing costs for a daylong conference; purchasing T-shirts for students who are providing a new library service—these are just a few ways small funds can have greater impacts. For larger operations, a library offering between $500 to $5,000 awards can go a long way toward inspiring the submission of highly innovative, competitive grant proposals. Such awards can cover the cost of external graphic designers or programmers for the production of websites or infographic materials; digitizing primary sources; or purchasing devices for transcribing or recording oral histories.

How Many Applications Can an Individual Submit?

Limiting the number of submissions by a project director in any given grant cycle may be an important way to encourage diverse participation. It can be challenging to lead more than one project at a time while maintaining responsibility for regular duties. Serving on multiple project teams while leading just one project may be the answer for libraries with smaller pools of librarians and staff. Another consideration to be included in the guidelines may be to limit a project idea to a single submission. Mini-grant programs should discourage recurring requests for funding of projects that are identical to those previously awarded. Applicants can be encouraged to expand or alter a previously awarded project so as to make a new application sufficiently unique in order to meet this eligibility requirement.

What Will Be the Annual Deadline(s) and Grant Period(s) for Application Submissions?

Answering this question may depend on a given library's fiscal year start and end dates. For instance, a deadline of May 15 gives a committee sufficient review time to award projects that begin after July 1. This works well if the library's fiscal year begins July 1 as it can allow project directors twelve months to complete their project prior to the end of the fiscal year. If a library chooses to offer two annual deadlines for internally funded proposals, then other possible deadlines may be October 1 with projects beginning after November 15 and prior to November 20; or the deadline could be January 15 with projects beginning after March 1, thus avoiding the holidays and the new year in both scenarios. Suppose a larger library has decided to offer two mini-grant application cycles and the first deadline is October 1; then the second deadline could be May 1 to give prospective applicants more time to plan grant projects. The grants committee's consideration of workload, events, holidays, vacations, and other similar occurrences can contribute to removing those timing barriers for successfully operating an internal funding program. Typically grant periods are no shorter than one year, which generally will give project directors sufficient time to complete their awarded projects.

How Will Applications Be Evaluated?

Reviewing the evaluation criteria for just a few external sponsors is a good way to identify appropriate criteria. Application completeness and budget feasibility are standard criteria for small grants programs. Other criteria typically include degree of innovation; significance to furthering the library's mission and goals; degree to which time frame and project objectives can be met; and potential for replication or long-term sustainability.

These are just a few examples. Each criterion should provide a range of points—one to five or one to ten, for instance—to allow reviewers to match the criteria with the quality of specific application attributes. For example, the committee can choose four criteria, each valued at up to five points. The total number of possible points per application can be twenty. Each committee member can allocate scores for each criterion. Then combining and averaging the numbers for each application, the committee can view the order of application scores and determine whether applications that don't meet a minimum standard—say, less than an average score of fifteen or sixteen—are declined. Those achieving the minimum average score or higher can then be ranked for award allocation, thereby determining which projects will receive total or partial funding.

How Can the Application Guidelines Frame a Mini-Grant Program That Rewards Projects for Including Collaborative Partners?

Most external sponsor guidelines include provisions for applicant contributions or "matching funds" provided by the applicant. Quite often the contribution is provided through time and effort of currently funded professionals whose percentage of salary and fringe benefits for contributed time and effort can be calculated and presented as matching funds. Other terms for this type of contribution are "cost share" (most often used in academic institutions) or "in-kind" contributions (used in the nonprofit sector). By requiring the contribution of a small percentage of cost share from a library professional other than the project director, the grants committee can discourage submissions of "solo" projects from being eligible. For instance, if a project application requests $2,500 in mini-grant funding, the committee might want to require that an additional 10 or 20 percent of the requested amount be contributed as cost share or effort provided by librarians or library staff in addition to what the project director plans to contribute.

Another option for the grants committee is to add merit to those applications that create innovative collaborations or partnerships with external entities or scholars. A scoring criterion that rates/evaluates the quality of cooperative, coordinative, or collaborative elements of a project also can enhance the incentive to work with other individuals or new entities toward the successful completion of a project. The committee should strive to reward applicants who genuinely and deliberately combine forces with others as a means for developing institutional skills in this regard.

How Does the Committee Deal with "Conflicts of Interest" during the Review Process?

A conflict of interest can occur in any grant review environment, especially within a library. Reviewers should disclose their potential conflict prior to the review of applications to discuss whether the committee members feel that an actual conflict of interest exists. For instance, the committee may determine that if a mini-grant lead or colead applicant also is a reviewer, then all discussion and scoring should occur while the reviewer with a conflict is not present. If a reviewer is included in an application only as part of the project team, this situation may not rise to the level of a conflict of interest as long as the reviewer feels that he or she can judge the merit of other applications objectively without unfairly favoring his or her own project.

Other conflicts of interest can be present in the application itself. Consider the situation where a librarian has requested mini-grant funds to contract a graphic design consultant. The applicant is awarded funds for this purpose and later hires his or her spouse as the consultant who will report directly to the applicant during the project grant period. Provisions should be included in the guidelines to deter this type of conflict of interest scenario that may occur after the project has been awarded.

What Information Should Mini-grant Applications Contain?

Using instructions and application components similar to those found in externally sponsored grant guidelines can ensure that librarians are receiving the most relevant grant preparation experience. A good list of mini-grant application contents might include these items: cover sheet form; project narrative and budget narrative questions; budget expenses form; and attachments including bibliography, letters of commitment, and letters of support that can accomplish this desired effect.

The textbox contains examples of the types of information, specified in guideline instructions, for fully completing a mini-grant proposal. This chart can be used as a starting template for adding or deleting elements to customize a library's mini-grant application content. Grant application documents usually include a

1. cover sheet form,
2. narrative (responses to specific project questions),
3. budget form,
4. budget narrative (responses to specific budget questions), and
5. attachments (bibliography, letters of commitment, and letters of support).

The textbox contains details of mini-grant content that can be used to design application requirements. For additional information, appendix 3.1 offers an example of mini-grant program guidelines.

Step 4: Coach Applicants and Project Team to Prepare Fundable Applications

Grants committee members along with other library staff should provide ways to assist potential applicants in developing fundable applications. This requires one-on-one mentoring in addition to group training sessions. A library has options for providing these services. It can hire an experienced grants coordinator (part-time or full-time depending on the number of librarians who are interested in pursuing grant opportunities) whose job includes managing the mini-grant process in coordination with the grants committee as well as assisting with external applications. If a coordinator is not on staff, any library employee or volunteer, including members of the grants committee with grant-writing experience, may be considered a viable provider of grant development advice. Grants committee members providing these services should simply disclose their involvement in the preparation of mini-grant proposals as a means for managing possible conflicts of interest (with other committee members). Potential grant applicants also should be encouraged to share drafts of their proposals with others, especially those completely ignorant of the project or the topic. Comments from these "editors" will help to ensure the proposal can be thoroughly understood by any prospective reviewers. A goal for applicants is to prepare proposals that can stand alone—meaning these proposals do not generate any unanswered questions, allowing reviewers sufficient information to make decisions simply on the merit of the application content.

SAMPLE GUIDELINE
COMPONENTS FOR A MINI-GRANT PROGRAM

1. Cover sheet form
   - Name of applicant and project team members
   - Project title
   - Amount requested
   - Amount of contributed cost share
   - Is this the applicant's first grant application?
   - Stakeholders/departments approving available resources to execute the project
   - Supervisor approval for project leader's effort contribution
2. Narrative instructions (three- to four-page limit)
   - What is the proposed project, its goals, objectives, and major activities?
   - How does the project support the library's mission and strategic plan?
   - What's the significance of the project to library patrons or other stakeholders?
   - How is the proposed project innovative?
   - How will the project be promoted?
   - What is the timeline that illustrates the work plan?
   - How will the project be sustained beyond the grant period?
3. Budget form
   - Personnel (temporary)
   - Consultant(s)
   - Travel (site visits, outreach, or promotion)
   - Supplies (could include food)
   - Equipment
   - Other
4. Budget narrative instructions (one-page limit)
   - For each line of the budget, what are the specific expenses needed to carry out the project as described in the schedule of completion?
   - How were the expense amounts determined and calculated?
   - Why are these expenses needed to complete the project?
5. Application attachments
   - Bibliography of works referenced in the narrative
   - Letters of commitment from those external to the project team and those external to the library who represent external organizational partners (if applicable)
   - Letters of support (no more than three) from those external to the project team who are knowledgeable about the project, can speak to its importance, and want to see it come to fruition

Preparing grant applications is not an individual sport. To be successful, the applicant must practice working with others on project planning. The applicant who is adept at facilitating cooperation, coordination, and sometimes collaboration with a variety of individuals is most likely to achieve the best possible proposal. While preparing a grant project, the project director is essentially functioning like the circus performer, juggling three bowling pins while keeping six plates spinning on sticks. Multiple conversations with various stakeholders, both internal and external to the library, will need to take place. While navigating these conversations and inquiring about available resources and potential project team members, the project director learns what is possible, including how to access resources, when to make requests for resources, and generally how best to relate with each resource owner in the thread of conversations—understanding his or her respective system of operations and workflows—and preparing a way forward if the proposal gets awarded.

An indispensable library partner in the project development process is the library's accountant. Working side by side with the accountant will ensure the project team's ideas for expenses—such as hiring temporary personnel, purchasing supplies or equipment, or contracting consultants—are sound, fit well within mini-grant guidelines, and can be executed easily by the accounting staff if the project is awarded. As awarded projects are managed, many minor as well as serious difficulties can be avoided by including the accountant in the preplanning of any grant proposal. When fiscal service members have a voice in making budget decisions, they essentially join the project as the budget development expert—facilitating decision making about project expenses from a place of expertise and access to financial information within the library's internal fiscal management systems, policies, and procedures. Good relationships with accountants can contribute greatly to the positive support for engaging in library grantsmanship activities. The last thing a project team wants is to learn about an expense that cannot be carried out as envisioned in the proposal, because of an unforeseen fiscal management rule or prerequisite.

Developing any fundable grant project is essentially a process of developing a project plan that aligns with the specific evaluation criteria embedded within the review guidelines. A mini-grant application can be expected to take, on average, forty hours to complete. Library administrators should acknowledge the importance of planning and writing proposals and should be committed to supporting those employees who choose to spend time in pursuit of grant funding. Salaried personnel may choose to contribute additional time beyond the workday to work on the proposal, but when hourly personnel also are involved in project planning and writing, some work duties or schedules will need to be adjusted to accommodate this additional time.

Those with little project development experience may find it challenging to know where to start. Hypothetically, let's say that the project idea is to set up a roving reference service within the library. The project originator has no experience managing such a service, but believes it is needed to meet a variety of situations and conditions that she has observed, such as: (1) few (especially younger) patrons taking advantage of the reference desk service, which is in obvious view with adequate signage; (2) an increase in laptop thefts when patrons leave their laptops unattended to seek reference services; (3) younger patrons believing they don't need the reference service because either they can access the information they need online; prefer not to have to talk to "strangers," especially "older" librarians; or they feel vulnerable because they don't know something or can't find the answer. In this case, a librarian wants to use mini-grant funds to cover the costs of testing a new library service: roving reference. Her vision of a roving reference service would be to assist patrons, especially those under the age of twenty-one, by implementing an easily accessible, peer-to-peer service while moving throughout the library, rather than remaining anchored to a reference desk.

A good way to start such a proposal is to find direct evidence to confirm the need for or viability of the proposed service, beyond collecting on-site observations of patron behavior. A survey of patrons under the age of twenty-one may provide additional information about why these patrons choose not to use the standard reference service and to determine the likelihood they would use a roving reference service if it were offered. Another way to gather evidence of project viability is to determine whether the method has been used or tested in other libraries. This can be achieved by conducting a literature review, posting the topic on a listserv or other interest group e-mail group system, or posting on a blog where others discuss library reference service issues.

If these inquiries continue to validate the worthiness of the project, then another step could be to convene library colleagues for a brainstorming session. Methodology developed by Brigham Young University (BYU) Office of Information Technology project planners has proven to be very effective in creating a friendly and engaging environment for sharing thoughts, comments, questions, and ideas about implementing a new project. This style of brainstorming was demonstrated by the managing director of enterprise project management, Ernie Nielsen, to library personnel during a project management training session at the University of Arizona Library in 2007. To use a slightly modified version of the BYU methodology for this purpose, first create a list of questions that will assist in both developing the project plan and answering the mini-grant application questions. Here are some examples of questions that might be used to brainstorm the roving reference service project idea:

- Do you think this is feasible? Why or why not?
- What will be the benefits of a pilot project?
- What types of customers would benefit?
- What types of technologies should be considered?
- What are some of the methods to evaluate this project?
- What time of day and during which semester time frame do you think this service should be offered and why?
- Who should train the students [rovers] and what should the training program include?
- What kinds of questions should we expect students [rovers] to answer? What kinds of questions are better referred to library staff?
- What supervision or monitoring methods might produce the best results for OPS [outside professional services/temporary employee] student workers providing these services?
- How should the pilot program be promoted?
- What risks should the project team be aware of? (What could go wrong?)

Next, invite everyone who works in the library, including volunteers, to participate and make sure to include a summary of the project idea in the invitation message. Not everyone will attend, of course, but the purpose of inviting everyone is to encourage inclusiveness, and to promote and expand the library's grant-seeking activities.

These sessions are usually thirty to forty-five minutes in length—it has been said that people can only brainstorm for about ten minutes before running out of steam. To prepare the space for the session, choose a room with lots of empty wall space. Write each question at the top of an easel paper and tape these papers to the walls, side by side, in some kind of numerical order.

After most participants have arrived, the owner of the idea presents a five-minute overview of the new project idea, its objectives, possible merits, and benefits. The idea owner then answers any questions about the project to clarify any confusion about the project idea. Next, participants each receive a stack of 3" × 3" sticky notes on which they will write their answers to the questions and stick them to the appropriate question page. Participants also have the option of initialing their sticky note for future contact to clarify or converse with the project idea owner. This activity provides many potential benefits:

- It creates a sense of community where others can freely contribute to an idea that may come to fruition.
- It creates project-planning transparency, making the idea a public topic for conversation in the library.
- It reveals hidden observations, opinions, resources, risks, solutions, collaborators, and so forth, that otherwise may have remained undiscovered.
- It gives those who are interested in the project a space and time to share their enthusiasm or skepticism with the idea owner.
- It provides a means for recruiting interested project team members.

After everyone has exhausted their contributions to the questions, there can be a casual debriefing, or the questions can remain posted in the room for sharing with others or to give those who could not attend the session the opportunity to provide feedback throughout the day. Here are excerpts from answers provided during a brainstorming session at the University of Florida Smathers Libraries for a proposed roving reference service project idea:

1. What will be the benefits of a pilot project?
   - Patrons' ability to access help when and where they need it
   - Ability of reference staff to prioritize user need as well as track and provide help where/when needed
   - Students will feel more connected—part of the process
   - Students that require assistance with finding books/printer problems/or even reference-related questions (like on Ask a Librarian)
   - Value-added service to students—good PR for library
   - Proactive, just-in-time service
   - A great way to try something without a 100 percent commitment
2. What types of customers would benefit?
   - Students place-bound, unable to locate materials
   - Lazy people, shy people, a few people who didn't think they needed help
   - All patrons—students in stacks or at broken equipment, or lost
   - Faculty, students all levels, visitors
   - I could see this benefiting anyone physically located in the building— students especially, since they like to "camp out" at tables
   - Maybe lots of students have questions but don't ask, don't wait in line for reference, or don't know where to turn

- Customers who have basic directional questions (e.g., finding a book, printer/computer problems) and maybe even reference-related questions
3. What types of technologies should be considered?
    - Support for tablets, support for use of large monitors (small groups)
    - Use existing "Ask a" toll-free number for UF Libraries
    - Phablets would make most sense
    - Tablet that can be taken to assist with any online needs, plus if the student could "drop a pin" as to their location then it could be used to locate them
    - Maybe iPads/netbooks to look up information (e.g., catalog, librarian info)
4. What are some of the methods to evaluate this project?
    - Online survey and a small incentive to give feedback
    - Keep stats on requests, feedback from staff and patrons
    - Obtain student/user e-mail and send a brief survey
    - Number of calls staff receives, number of problems resolved
    - Feedback from students/survey, numbers/stats
    - Three-question survey on tablet, usage stats/ref analytics in order to track
5. What time of day and during which semester time frame do you think this service should be offered and why?
    - Use gate counts to assess times of year when traffic is high and pilot the project at those times
    - Definitely during fall and spring regular hours to coincide with class/course schedule on campus
    - Try a two- to three-week period to test ideas
    - Definitely during finals
    - According to peak times of wastewater usage
    - Late afternoon/early evenings are probably the best time of day (seems that is when the library is most busy)
6. Who should train the students and what should the training program include?
    - Importance of referral
    - Sounds like circulation staff training primarily but maybe some librarian perspective as well
    - Main reference staff should train, IT should train on IT issues
    - Purpose/benefits how to handle each type of need, role-plays
7. What kinds of questions should we expect student workers to answer? What kinds of questions are better referred to library staff?
    - Basic reference directional, how to use OneSearch, EBSCO, some IT
    - Routine and usual questions (photocopying, scanning, locating books), any substantive or advanced questions need to go to reference staff
    - Same as was expected on circulation/reference desk
8. What supervision or monitoring methods might produce the best results for paid student workers providing these services?
    - Each student should be paired with a mentor, mentors should form a group to coordinate this
    - Either a circulation or reference person on call to help the helper
    - Training with branches and subject specialists
    - Semester evaluation, keep track of complaint/praise received
    - Subject librarian, meetings to talk about activities, performance, remediation
    - Questions and answers, role-play with supervisors

9. How should pilot program be promoted?
   - Tweets
   - OPS students wear T-shirts with phone number on front and back (or aprons)
   - Flyers, Sakai and Canvas, posters, professors
   - Social media, signage, formal marketing campaign
   - Ads or news article
   - Using social media (FB, Twitter, etc.), flyers, bookmarks, pens
   - Posters, flyers, banners
   - Faculty newsletter (graduate/postdoc)
   - Student body announcement
   - Promo on main web page event
   - On computer screens in the commons area
   - Library ambassadors, 3D printed phone number
   - Social media, business cards with snappy design, web page near Ask a Librarian service since students often use this for some purpose
10. What risks should the project team be aware of? (What could go wrong?)
    - Maybe encountering a "difficult" or frustrated user
    - Complaints or unruly patrons
    - Student reference assistants not making appropriate referrals
    - Misinformation
    - Frustration if not at time/speed students want
    - Too many/too few on to handle need by patrons
    - Challenge of three floors—need enough students to cover
    - Request that may be too complex for texting/brief message reply
    - No one uses it; mobile device gets broken

A result of the brainstorming session, beyond acquiring feedback and comments, valuable ideas, and questions, could be that the idea owner now has a list of possible project team members—either those who attended the session or those who were recommended as potential team members by session participants. Brainstorming session participants often make the best project team members: they have demonstrated (1) an interest in the topic, (2) knowledge to share about an aspect of the project, and (3) willingness to contribute time and effort. In terms of grants preparation, the project team must include individuals who are sincerely interested and knowledgeable in the topic, and who are committed to contributing effort to implement the project. With a list of prospective project team members and information from the brainstorming session, the project team is now equipped to flesh out a schedule of major activities, with corresponding suggestions for responsible parties to carry out these activities and complete the project. Table 3.1 is a sample timeline for implementing the fictitious roving reference mini-grant project.

The schedule of activities—sometimes referred to as the schedule of completion or timeline—should sufficiently detail the project such that a person completely ignorant of the project could visualize the implementation process, from start to finish, simply by reviewing it without any additional explanation. This type of detailed information forms the basis for creating the project budget. The budget basically articulates the schedule of activities in the form of expense categories and expense amounts required to carry out all proposed activities. It also includes the cost share, in the form of percent of effort (salary and fringe benefits for time related to executing the activities listed in the timeline) that

Table 3.1. Sample Timeline for the Roving Reference Mini-Grant Project

TIME FRAME	ACTIVITY	PERSON RESPONSIBLE
November 15 to January 15	Develop guidelines and protocols for the service Include: case scenarios; reporting structure; mentoring frameworks; survey method; debriefing system Design T-shirts and signage Design referral cards	Project director with team input and editing Communications director
January 15 to March 1	Develop schedule for service Purchase supplies/equipment Develop job description for student workers Recruit and hire student workers Train student workers Match students with mentors Complete printing	Project team IT coordinator Project director Student coordinator Team Student coordinator Communications director
February 15	Begin promoting pilot project	Team
March 1 to April 15	Launch pilot project Capture feedback; collect and process data	Team Student coordinator
April 15 /16	Interview students and mentors	Student coordinator
April 30	Produce evaluation report and findings	Project director
May 15 to June 15	Revise protocols based on evaluation findings Recruit and hire student workers Train students	Team Student coordinator Student coordinator
June 1	Promote project	Team
June 15 to August 1	Launch revised pilot project Capture feedback; collect and process data	Team
August 1/2	Interview students and mentors	Student coordinator
August 15	Produce evaluation report and findings	Project director
September 1	Revise protocols based on evaluation findings	Team
September 30	Compile results from two tests	Project director
November 30	Prepare final report for mini-grant and determine whether further development of the program is of interest to library administration	Project director

library employees plan to contribute. Table 3.2 is a contrived sample budget for completing the fictitious roving reference mini-grant project within a twelve-month grant period:

With the availability of draft budget information, the project team now can determine whether the project is feasible. Assessing project feasibility is, without a doubt, the most important step in a grant-planning process. It provides the project team with a method to examine whether the team should proceed to plan and write all the remaining components of the application to meet the deadline at hand. Is more information needed? Can the project be fully developed in time to meet the deadline without making unrealistic demands on the project team? Can submission of the application be delayed? Or does the timing of the deadline require that the project be abandoned? Is the project

Table 3.2. Sample Budget for the Roving Reference Mini-Grant Project

EXPENSE CATEGORY AND DETAIL	EXPENSE AMOUNT	CONTRIBUTED COST SHARE
Personnel:		
Lisa Gonzalez: project director, reference librarian (5%)		$2,000
Frank Smith, social sciences librarian (3%)		$1,200
Melody Rice, student coordinator (10%)		$3,000
Bill Dean, communications coordinator (1%)		$400
Subtotal Personnel	–0	$6,600
OPS:		
Student Labor, 3 students @ $8/hour x 8 hours/week x 10 weeks x 2 phases	$3,840	
Subtotal OPS	$3,840	–0
Supplies:		
Signage printing (5) (Target Copy donation)		$100
T-shirts (6) (KJ Printing donation)		$60
Subtotal Supplies	–0	$160
Equipment:		–0
3 iPad mini tablets	$900	
3 mobile phones	$240	
Subtotal Equipment	$1,140	–0
Total Cash Request	$4,980	
Total Cost Share		$6,760
Total Project Cost	$11,740	

too costly in comparison with anticipated benefits; is it a redundant service; or would the proposal not score well vis-à-vis the criteria for evaluating mini-grants? Project owners should welcome the opportunity to consider the feasibility of their project—especially knowing that members of the project team want to be part of a worthwhile endeavor. Few people are likely to be interested in spending many hours of effort to develop a project plan and subsequent grant proposal if the likelihood of failure is unreasonably high. If the project is deemed feasible, the project team can proceed with confidence that their efforts will likely bear fruit.

One way to determine the feasibility of a mini-grant project plan is for the applicant to meet with the grants coordinator, if one exists, or any of the grants committee members prior to developing the project narrative section of the application. Committee members may have experience in evaluating previous grant proposals and will likely have insights into ways to strengthen the proposal plan or to reduce or expand budget items to improve the quality of the project. They may recommend that simply dividing the number of potential beneficiaries into the total cost of the project will yield a cost per beneficiary. If the cost is deemed to be too high, then the project team can see that the project is impractical and likely to be declined.

For example, in the roving reference project budget scenario, students are proposed to work for ten weeks at eight hours per week for two different phases—the first phase plans to test the roving reference concept with newly hired student workers, and the second plans to adjust the process by which students communicate with patrons based on patron feedback during the first phase. A grants committee member might suggest that the initial time frame for phase I may be too long because sufficient information can be gathered after four weeks of testing the service rather than ten weeks. Other questions related to determining feasibility would include: Can funding for this project or some of its activities come from other readily available sources? Can the project be completed without submitting a mini-grant proposal? Does the project idea sufficiently match the guidelines? Can the project be realistically completed within the grant period? These questions can become the basis for a meaningful discussion about the project, often yielding unexpected creative ideas for expanding innovation, leveraging unique resources, or benefiting more constituents.

Another important step in the process of determining project feasibility is to share the project plan and budget with those library personnel whose workflow or workload may be impacted if the project is awarded. It is always best to ensure project plans have been shared and vetted with project team member supervisors and those potentially impacted by the project. It should be the project owner's goal to convey project plans so as to avoid surprising library personnel with additional work responsibilities, deadlines, or other types of unspoken expectations.

At the point when mini-grant projects have been assessed to be feasible by various library personnel not serving on the project team, the team can proceed with confidence to distribute responsibilities, among themselves, for completing the application requirements and finalizing the schedule of activities and budget. The project team should create a mini-grant application checklist—customized for the roving reference project while using the requirements stated in the guidelines—to guide them and ensure that they complete all application components. It is, of course, imperative that all review criteria be fully addressed within the application. These sample criteria can be used to illustrate the process of developing a customized checklist:

- Application completeness (maximum five points)
- Level of uniqueness and evidence of innovation (maximum ten points)
- Potential impact on the library's patrons and stakeholders (maximum ten points)
- Evidence the project can be completed successfully (maximum ten points)

For the purpose of sharing a hypothetical customized checklist, consider that the application guidelines include requirements such as: cover sheet, four-page narrative, budget, budget narrative, bibliography, letters of commitment from library (other than project team) and partner organization(s) staff, no more than two letters of support from individuals (different from letters of commitment authors) who can speak with authority about the value of the project, and no more than five pages of attachments providing additional information. Using the roving reference project as an example along with the sample criteria and grant guidelines, table 3.3 presents a checklist to help guide the project director and team in completing the application package.

With the completion of the customized mini-grant checklist, the project team is now prepared to begin writing and gathering information. It may seem to the reader that there are too many steps to complete prior to actually writing the application, thus making the

Table 3.3. Checklist for Guiding the Preparation of the Roving Reference Mini-grant Proposal

MINI-GRANT REQUIREMENTS AND REVIEW CRITERIA	NOTES	PERSON(S) RESPONSIBLE FOR PREPARING CONTENT
Cover sheet with project title, summary, team members, amount requested, approvals to access available resources, amount and source of cost share	Make a list of all departments involved to get signature approvals.	Project director
Narrative requirements—4 pages single spaced, 1" margins, 11 pt. font	*Create a list of required questions to be answered.*	*Determine who will be involved in preparing proposal.*
1) What is the proposed project, funding request, goals, objectives, and major activities?	Finalize this section last.	Project director
2) How does the project support the library's mission and strategic plan?	Project team input; review library mission/plan to tie project to mission and plan.	Project director
3) What is the significance of the project to library patrons or other stakeholders? How will patrons and other stakeholders benefit from the project?	Literature review, online searching for similar projects; make a list of all those to benefit and their respective benefits.	Social sciences librarian
4) How is the proposed project innovative? What evidence is available to confirm project innovativeness? How does the project compare and contrast, in terms of uniqueness, to other similar projects?	Literature review, online searching for similar projects; post questions to library blogs or listservs; create bibliography.	Social sciences librarian
5) What are the activities and corresponding timeline for executing the project? What evidence exists that validates the timeline and activities can be completed in one year?	List participant skills and experience; use past successful project completion evidence.	Project director and social sciences librarian
6) How do you propose to promote the project?	Find methods for successfully promoting new patron services in the library and in the literature.	Project director, social sciences librarian, and communications coordinator

Deliverable / Question	Instructions	Responsible
7) How will the project be sustained beyond the grant period?	This one can be tricky if the project is a proof of concept or involves research or planning. Consider how best to answer if there will be plans to continue any of the project deliverables.	Project team
Timeline illustrating the work plan	Make a list of all activities to complete the project. (Do this step first.)	Project team members
Budget (one page)	Use the timeline as a guide to complete the mini-grant application budget form. (This is the second step.)	Project director and accountant
Budget narrative or justification for expenses (one page)	Gather expense info from vendors of supplies and equipment, and outside consulting fees planned for the project. (Do this in conjunction with the budget form.)	Project director
Letters (or e-mails) of commitment from those outside the project team who are actively involved in the project and work in the library	Make a list of all those planning to commit to participate in the project; create e-mail message request with instructions for letter writers. (Do this after timeline and budget have been completed—early in the preparation process.)	Project director and communications coordinator
Letters (or e-mails) of commitment from those partnering organization(s) representatives actively involved in the project	Make a list of all partnering organizations and contacts; create e-mail message with request/instructions for letter writers. (Do this after timeline and budget have been completed—early in the preparation process.)	Project director and communications coordinator
Letters (or e-mails) of support (no more than three) from those who will enthusiastically support the project and can speak credibly about its positive impact on the library, stakeholders, community, or the field strengthened by the project	Invite the most knowledgeable people working in reference services and with young patrons, who are not employed by the library. (Do this after timeline and budget have been completed—early in the preparation process.)	Project director and communications coordinator

process cumbersome and drawn out. This is one reason why project directors and teams will need encouragement from grants committee members and library administrators to follow the steps outlined in this chapter if they aspire to build a collaborative grant-seeking environment in their library. These steps in actuality will save grant-seekers many hours of anguish and frustration. Cutting corners such as eliminating project planning or feasibility assessment processes ultimately will reduce the quality of project proposals. Even worse, these actions can sabotage the library's grant-seeking program by having teams spend tens of hours writing proposals that aren't feasible, lack continuity from the budget to the narrative and the timeline, or ignore the criteria for evaluating proposal quality.

Because libraries are first and foremost service providers, library employees often struggle to find time to prepare fundable grant projects. Consequently, project teams may be tempted to write proposals without first planning and assessing the feasibility of ideas and activities that frame them. Succumbing to this temptation can fritter away their time and cause great harm to a grant-seeking program, ultimately producing many declined proposals. Inevitably if a library receives too many declinations, relative to awarded grants, the culture of grantsmanship will suffer.

On the other hand, once preparing grants using these planning methods becomes commonplace over time, librarians and library staff together will become increasingly efficient and proficient at generating any type of grant proposal. Regardless of the topic or the vagueness of the sponsor's guidelines, librarians who have practiced these methods will have developed the confidence and know-how to determine the feasibility of pursuing a grant opportunity or the good sense to choose not to waste anyone's time in the pursuit of projects that are not feasible—either from the viewpoint of the library's project team or the prospective sponsor.

In diligently preparing the application, project directors and team members will achieve various learning outcomes from their involvement. For a snapshot outlining some sample narrative questions and correlating learning outcomes, see table 3.4.

On the day following the mini-grants application submission deadline, all applications can be delivered to reviewers either electronically, if proposals were submitted as PDFs (the preferred file format), or in printed versions. The grants committee will meet twice during the review: once within one week of the application deadline and a second time within three weeks of the first meeting.

During the first meeting, grants committee members will not evaluate the merit of applications. Because the purpose of the mini-grants program is to train applicants who are new to grant-seeking protocols or to encourage experienced grant-seekers to practice their skills, the committee should resist any inclination to assign merit or to find fault with the quality of proposals at the first meeting. Instead, after reviewing applications, the committee brainstorms a list of questions that, when answered, will provide a more complete picture of each proposed project. The applicant's imperative goal always should be to provide sufficient and clear information about the project to the extent that reviewers will have no questions. This sets the bar quite high in terms of striving to produce the most complete application within the space constraints imposed by the guidelines while answering all of the imagined questions reviewers might have.

The list of questions prepared at the first review meeting essentially provides feedback to applicants about where the application falls short of its desired outcome: no reviewer questions. The goal of reviewers in these localized library environments is to gather the answers to their questions, thus closing the gap on any missing information that may prevent reviewers from adequately evaluating the quality of the project idea, the execution

Table 3.4. Example Learning Outcomes Resulting from Preparing Mini-Grant Proposals

SAMPLE MINI-GRANT NARRATIVE QUESTIONS	LEARNING OUTCOMES FOR APPLICANTS
What is the proposed project, its goals, objectives, and major activities?	Honing the project idea into a succinct summary to engage the reader's interest and stimulate visual imagery about the project idea and expected results
How much is the applicant seeking and for what expense purpose?	Working with the timeline to determine all related expenses, and requesting a specific dollar amount (not a range) that articulates the purpose for which funds will be used
How does the project support the library's mission and strategic plan?	Discovering how the project can benefit the library's future goals
What's the significance of the project to library patrons or other stakeholders?	Defining the importance of the project by examining types of potential benefits created by the project not just for those directly benefiting, but also for multiple constituents served by partnering entities, and the library staff members themselves
How is the proposed project innovative?	Finding evidence of project innovativeness, comparing the project to other similar endeavors at other libraries, and making a case for the value of the project's uniqueness and sustainability
How do you plan to promote the project?	Learning and tapping into others' knowledge about ways to promote such a project
What are the activities and corresponding timeline for executing the project?	Learning or practicing basic project-planning skills especially in describing activities and time frames that create dependencies and constraints with multiple project team members in various departments
If this is a digitization project, who owns the collection and what are the copyright issues?	Learning about copyright limitations, workflow requirements, and procedures to acquire permissions
Building a bibliography	Locating and referencing evidence in the literature, online or from other sources, that supports the case for uniqueness, innovation, targeted audience needs, possible impacts, or other benefits provided in the narrative
Acquiring letters of commitment and acquiring letters of support	Creating written and oral requests that build buy-in from external project sources and result in convincing and unique letters of commitment and support from letter writers

and promotion plan, its innovativeness, and all of the other appropriate review criteria. Once all of the questions have been answered by the applicant/project director in cooperation with project team members, and shared with the reviewers, the grants committee can proceed to convene the second meeting to assign scores and determine funding. This methodology provides each applicant with the opportunity to fully complete the application to the best of his or her ability, allowing all applications to be reviewed for merit on a more equal basis.

After the applicants have received the reviewers' questions and have been allotted sufficient time to draft their responses, the committee coordinates individual meetings with each applicant and a committee member. The applicant project director may bring other team members to the meeting if that might be helpful. At the beginning of the meeting, the committee representative provides an overview of the review process and makes the applicant aware that the committee has not yet addressed the merit of any proposals. During the meeting, the applicant and committee representative review the draft of the applicant's answers to the committee's questions. The representative reads the answer to each question and discusses ways that the answers might have more effectively answered the committee's questions, concerns, or confusions.

This is repeated with each applicant in a relatively short time frame. Each applicant should be given the same amount of time to prepare answers and, if recommended by the representative, provide additional information. There should be no restrictions on the amount of information the applicant may want to provide as long as it is reasonable and doesn't require extensive time to review. All of the applicants' questions are then collated into a single document for reviewers. On rare occasions, there may be instances where reviewers completely understand the entire application and no additional information is needed to allow for a thorough review of the project.

Prior to the second meeting, the grants committee members should take time to reread all the applications along with the new information delivered from applicants. During this second review, they also assign scores using a score sheet delineating the title of each application, list of criteria, maximum points for each criterion, and a place to write notes and rationale for scores, based on each criterion as described in the application guidelines.

At the beginning of the second meeting, reviewers first agree to treat all the information exchanged during the meeting as confidential. It is imperative that applicants don't learn about the opinions of reviewers through means outside the formal review process. Any reviewer with a perceived conflict of interest should make this disclosure. Provisions should be made to accommodate these conflicts if the committee deems this to be necessary. After a review of the procedures for scoring and discussing applications, each member discloses his or her assigned scores, which are then recorded on an electronic spreadsheet and projected on a screen so that everyone can check the accuracy of scores as they are entered and displayed. After all of the scores have been recorded for the first application, reviewers are encouraged to share comments about the application and explain the rationale for their own assigned scores. The discussion of application merit may convince some reviewers to change their scores. This can be achieved easily by using the electronic spreadsheet. All of the scores are then averaged and final scores are determined. Averaging adjusts for situations when the number of reviewers is not the same for all applications, due to conflicts of interest or absenteeism. The process is repeated until all applications have been scored and discussed, and decisions have been finalized.

At this point, the committee is faced with its responsibility to decide which proposal(s) should receive funding and at what levels. This process of allocating award funds differs in every application cycle as the number of applications and amount of requests will be unique to each cycle. The committee has the option to decline project proposals that don't meet the minimum average score requirement—for example, if the maximum number of points is twenty, the minimum average score requirement for funding awards could be fifteen. Committee members have the options of declining applications or of partially or fully funding proposal requests depending on the final scores and the amount of money available for granting. When all the funding decisions have been made, the committee prepares a document that includes the funding requests, project titles and abstract summaries, project director and project team members, final average score, and the committee's funding recommendation amounts and declinations for each project proposal. The document is then reviewed by the senior administrators who may want to pose questions to the committee for further clarification of project descriptions, rationale, or decisions. This may create changes in the committee's recommendations.

When all decisions are finalized and approved, a committee member prepares a letter of award or declination as appropriate for each applicant. Letters are signed by the chair of the committee or the director of the library and delivered to the applicant. It is best to share the score assigned to the applicant's proposal, the proposal ranking, and, if the proposal was declined, a brief description of the rationale for the declination outlining missing information and recommendations for how the proposal idea could be improved, using a very nonjudgmental tone.

Since the entire mini-grant proposal development and review process is intended to train future grant-seekers or to provide practice opportunities for experienced grant-writers, it is important to always be kind and encouraging to applicants and potential applicants. Committee members should resist any urge to share their proposal review comments. These comments may contain petty criticisms directed at the style of the application as opposed to the quality of the project idea and/or the schedule of completion plan for actualizing the idea. It should be noted that internal library grant reviewers do not serve anonymously—they are known and acknowledged for their service on the grants committee. Because of this transparency, sharing reviewer comments with applicants can be very harmful to a library's goal of building grant-seeking capacities. Reviewer comments, even for funded projects, may have the unintended consequence of causing resentment and negativity toward the reviewers and the review process. Unlike internal grantmaking committees, reviewers for externally sponsored grant review processes often provide individual reviewer comments to grant applicants as part of the review process, and in addition to award or declination letters. This is an effective means for sharing the views of anonymous reviewers that often leads to improvements in revised or future applications for funding. It avoids the possible harmful effects of reviewer comments that come from the opinions of one's library colleagues.

Finally, after all of the applicants have learned about the fate of their respective proposals, a general announcement is made to all library staff. The announcement should share information only about funded projects, including the title, project director and project team members, summary description, and awarded amount. Again, the goal here is to celebrate the achievements of those who submitted fundable proposals while avoiding any negative fallout for those whose applications were declined.

Step 6: Support Awarded Teams to Achieve Successful Project Completion

Following mini-grant award notifications, the committee or the grants coordinator should be prepared to provide training for and support to project directors and teams as they prepare to actualize their mini-grant projects. Assuming wrongly that project teams have the required "common sense" to carry out grant projects successfully can cause the library innumerable problems. For librarians with little or no grant or project management experience, the process of managing a project can be daunting. Because the management of grant projects and projects in general is reliant on the wisdom, commitment, resources, and energy of people, it can be an exciting journey as well as one fraught with unanticipated logistical and otherwise complex challenges.

Once the grants have been awarded but before the team starts work on the project, the committee would be well advised to coordinate an orientation workshop for all awardees, including all project directors and appropriate team members. Grant projects that begin with an orientation session about fiscal, human resource (HR), and grants management procedures for both planned activities and unexpected contingencies will start on a more solid foundation. Forming a partnership at the start to include the project director and team along with professionals managing fiscal and HR departments will provide an invaluable first step in executing the project as intended. Systems for tracking and expending funds for mini-grant projects will need to be developed to support project directors as they manage their budgets. This can be achieved by distributing monthly reports of expenditures as compared to the awarded application budget. Reports, which include projections as to how funds will be expended according to pay periods, can be very useful if temporary staff members are to be hired during the project. If personnel are needed for projects, it also will be important to create methods to assist mini-grant teams in developing position descriptions for these temporary staff, and also for recruiting, interviewing, hiring, and supervising students or temporary workers. Other preparation may be necessary for facilitating the purchase of mini-grant-funded equipment, based on existing library protocols for carrying out this type of activity. If the project involves enhancing the library's space, facilities department staff may want to develop policies and procedures for supporting small projects of this nature.

Project directors and project team members can benefit greatly from training sessions provided jointly by facilities, HR, and fiscal services departments in the context of managing grant-funded projects. Possible topics to be covered during a combined orientation session would typically include

- a review of processes for approving and tracking budget expenditures;
- methods for recruiting and hiring temporary staff;
- methods of contracting with consultants;
- obtaining bids for outside professional services or equipment; and
- booking travel and travel-related expenses.

The orientation workshop should include training related to understanding and avoiding conflicts of interest in hiring and contracting activities; extending a project if it can't be completed during the grant period; making changes to the budget line items; and supervising temporary staff and consultants. Training sessions that bring together all awarded project directors in the same grant cycle also provide a forum for sharing expertise and building camaraderie among those who are concurrently beginning new grant-funded projects.

Another topic for training sessions is reporting requirements. The grants committee must have a system for monitoring the expenditures of grants as well as tracking progress in completing activities listed in the timeline. This can be achieved through quarterly or six-month interim reports prepared by the project director and submitted to the grants committee for periodic review during the grant period. The committee will want to know

1. whether the project timeline presented in the proposal is still valid, or whether accommodations must be made;
2. whether the project is anticipated to end within the grant period or whether a "no-cost extension" may be necessary;

3. the categories and amounts of expenditures to date; and,
4. whether any changes have been made, especially to project team members, personnel, or in the expected products resulting from the project.

The content of these reports should be similar to or consistent with reporting requirements for external sponsors.

Reports can serve an important function in revealing the need for project or technical assistance. For example, a report can reveal these types of project discrepancies: no funds have been dispersed and the project is close to its end date; the IT employee on the project team has retired and no substitute has been planned; or the budget to date indicates all funds for travel have been expended, yet additional travel is necessary to complete the project. By learning of these situations through an interim report, the committee can strategize how best to assist the project director and team to prevent serious harm to the project. Reports provide a window into project activities that might not otherwise be available. Inexperienced project directors sometimes feel the need to withhold information if project issues appear to be without a solution or minor in nature. Requiring reports from all awardees helps to ensure periodic communication during the project while time remains available to make any necessary adjustments or interventions.

Committee members should anticipate that project teams will experience change to some extent. Being prepared to assist a project team should be something the committee plans for in advance. In lieu of a grants coordinator, the committee can opt to match a mini-grant project with a committee member to facilitate more frequent communication between the project director and its sponsor. Further, a final report due within thirty days of the project end date should include total expenditures for each line item, narrative or a chart describing completed activities, evaluation results, and information about outcomes and outputs resulting from the project.

With the completion of the mini-grant project management training/orientation session, project directors and teams now are ready to launch projects. To ensure a solid start, a kickoff meeting should be hosted for each project team. If the library employs a grants coordinator, then this person should be included. At the kickoff meeting the project director reviews project activities and expected results (products and outcomes). Each project team member then describes his or her respective role. The project director reviews reporting requirements, and time is allowed to discuss questions that need clarification or further attention beyond the meeting. A project director should never assume that this meeting is unnecessary, even if the project team consists of two people. The value of clarifying the context and activities of the project within this new period of time cannot be overemphasized. A kickoff meeting completion means the project has officially begun.

⑥ Examples of Awarded Mini-grant Projects at the University of Florida Libraries

In 2006, the George A. Smathers Libraries, encompassing nine libraries at the University of Florida, launched the Mini Grant Program. The impetus to establish the program was generated from the grant-writing successes achieved by a small staff in the Digital Library Center beginning in 1998. In 2004, a small group of librarians and curators convened to determine whether an internal grantmaking program could contribute to expanding this success for other library departments. The Mini Grant Program officially began awarding grants in 2006. The program was funded in 2008 at $25,000 for one annual grant cycle, with a deadline in October. Another cycle with an additional $25,000 allocation and a new deadline in May began in 2012. The Libraries' Grants Management Committee, with professional support from the grants manager, functions to oversee the program in the fashion outlined in the steps for creating and managing an internal grant-making program detailed in this chapter. The committee members include representatives from the Social Sciences Library, Marston Science Library, Special Collections and Area Studies, IT, Digital Production Services, Cataloging, and Fiscal Services Departments.

At the date of this writing, the Smathers Libraries program has sponsored fifty-three awards through $203,588 in internal library funding, and another thirteen applications have been declined. In the past six years, more than seventy library personnel have participated in projects funded by Mini Grants and external sponsors. The continued allocation of funds for this program by the dean of the Libraries, Judith Russell, has been indispensable in retaining systems for practicing grants preparation activities.

Each Mini Grant–awarded project evolved to produce stories of the project team's journey to actualize proposal plans and accompanying outcomes. Over time, new projects and surprising stories and unexpected events and connections developed as outgrowths of these previous Mini Grant awards. The Mini Grant Program has produced a portfolio of projects at Smathers Libraries that have been matches for continued funding by an endowment, opportunities for recycling successful resources to other projects, or the beginnings of much larger projects supported by external sponsors. Here are some examples.

GatorScholar

"GatorScholar: Developing a Database to Foster Interdisciplinary Communication and Collaboration at UF" was the brainchild of Valrie Minson and Sara Russell Gonzalez, librarians at the Marston Science Library. While attending a conference in Ithaca, New York, hosted by Cornell University, Minson learned of VIVO, a search engine developed by librarians and programmers at Cornell University Library. Gonzalez had been creating lists of publications authored by UF faculty in the Astronomy, Physics, and Geology Departments. A short time after the conference, Minson was given the opportunity to present information about the VIVO model to faculty at UF's Institute of Food and Agricultural Sciences (IFAS). It was here that the VIVO model received its original endorsement. Minson and Gonzalez codeveloped the idea to collaborate with VIVO's creators and IFAS faculty in replicating the system at UF. This summary describes their project as written in the Mini Grant application:

> This proposal requests funding to implement VIVO, a tool with the ability to improve access to faculty publications and to strengthen communication channels between departments, colleges and the library. VIVO is a search engine created by Cornell University Libraries and displays faculty and department information harvested from a variety of sources. The seed funds ($5,000) received from the Mini Grant will be used to hire one student assistant to input data for a select number of departments. Once populated, VIVO will serve as a promotional tool to recruit campus support, as well as allow the Libraries to explore the dynamic harvesting of data. (Minson and Gonzalez, 2007: 1)

During the grant period from 2007 through 2008, the VIVO project team received training from Cornell librarians, and set up and implemented the system, thus cumulating and loading faculty information to GatorScholar—UF's version of VIVO—focusing on agricultural faculty researchers and their respective areas of expertise, publications, and awarded grant proposals as a starting point. Michael Conlon, PhD, associate director and chief operating officer of the UF Clinical and Translational Science Institute (CTSI), became interested in the potential for GatorScholar as the tool he had been seeking for exposing CTSI's faculty assets. He later mused whether VIVO could be a possible platform for building collaborative relationships within and across disciplines in response to the National Institutes of Health's American Recovery and Reinvestment Act (ARRA) call for applications to design a national collaborative system.

In partnership with Minson and the Libraries' grants manager, Conlon, along with teams at Cornell University Library, and five other academic libraries (Washington University; Scripps Research Institute, La Jolla; Indiana University; Ponce School of Medicine, Puerto Rico; Weill Medical College of Cornell University, New York, New York), developed and submitted a proposal to NIH in 2009 titled "VIVO: Enabling National Networking of Scientists."

> The proposed work will establish a national networking of scientists by providing a new software system (VIVO) and support for scientists using VIVO. Scientists using VIVO will be able to find other scientists and their work. Conversely, scientists using VIVO will be found by other scientists doing similar or complimentary [sic] work. VIVO leverages work done over the past five years by Cornell University, supporting researchers and finding of researchers by representing data about them and their activities including publications, awards, presentations and partners. VIVO is fully extensible and based on Semantic Web concepts insuring sound data representation, vastly improved search over existing text based methods and integration of data with other applications. Support for researchers using VIVO will be done by librarians of the research institutions. Librarians provide an existing and fully integrated resource for enabling researchers and the national network. (Conlon, 2009: 3)

The NIH reviewers selected only one national project; UF and its partners were the recipients. A distinguishing element of the proposal, which may have influenced NIH reviewers, was the intent to center the project within academic libraries at each of the six partnering institutions rather than hosting the project in campus information technology units. Based on the previous VIVO systems at Cornell and UF, this model appeared to be unique, feasible, and competitive. Project team members at UF and partner institutions believed in the potential for leveraging the libraries' inherent assets: outreach expertise, extant relationships with faculty, and established trust in the areas of organization and dissemination of information. These combined assets, which were consistent within each participating academic partner for developing a community of contributors to and users of a national version of VIVO, made a strong case for selecting UF. The NIH award totaled over $12 million, of which $1.6 million was awarded to Smathers Libraries for outreach and implementation services.

As this example illustrates, a very small proof-of-concept project can take on grander forms when shared with others. Cornell University librarians and programmers wanted VIVO to be replicated at other sites. UF's unique combination of enthusiasm for VIVO and leadership experience in acquiring NIH grant awards became the catalyst that unlocked its national potential. No one can predict the ultimate impact of a $5,000 investment in a library idea. VIVO is now hosted by over fifty VIVO implementation sites in the United States, and VIVO projects are happening in over twenty-five countries.

Unearthing Historic St. Augustine

In 2010, the assistant head of the Architecture and Fine Arts Library, Tom Caswell, submitted the Mini Grant proposal "Historic St. Augustine Block and Lot Files" and received $5,000. The summary of the proposal states:

> This proposal requests funds to digitize the majority (85%) of the Historic St. Augustine Block and Lot Files. Started in the early 1960s, the files provided historical information to guide Historic St. Augustine Preservation Board administrators in the purchase and development of the colonial town and properties. Documents include historic interpretation notes, architectural sketches, drawings, archaeological field reports, maps, and photographs related to historic St. Augustine. The materials are of particular interest to researchers in architecture, historical archaeology, museum studies, tourism studies, historic preservation and restoration, as well as to those generally interested in the history of St. Augustine. (Caswell, 2008: 1)

Digital access to these hidden resources stored in Government House (in St. Augustine) drew major interest from the city's leaders of historical societies and preservation departments. Conversations among these stakeholders, the Libraries' Special and Area Studies curator of the P. K. Yonge Library of Florida History, and the curator of the Architecture Archives resulted in a National Endowment for the Humanities (NEH) proposal titled "Unearthing St. Augustine's Colonial Heritage: An Interactive Digital Collection for the Nation's Oldest City." In May 2012, the project received a $265,000 NEH grant award. The summary shares a window into the scope of the project:

> In preparation for St. Augustine's 450th Anniversary of its founding in 2015, the University of Florida (UF) Libraries requests $321,653 (with $196,821 in contributed cost share) to build an online collection of key resources related to research on colonial St. Augustine, Florida. Along with the UF Libraries, Unearthing St. Augustine partners are the two City of St. Augustine departments (Heritage Tourism and Archeology Program), historic Government House in St. Augustine managed by UF, and St. Augustine Historical Society. This two-year project will produce two major outcomes: 1) UF and its partners will establish for the first time a digitization computer lab at Government House which will be used to create and disseminate an interactive digital collection consisting of 11,000 maps, drawings, photographs and documents and associated metadata that will be available freely online; 2) project staff will spatially enhance digitized paper maps and images through a process called geo-referencing and create original programming to produce a user-friendly, Google map–based interface, and release it as open source technology. These products will allow for downloading and manipulating primary source material thus creating a means for increasing interactivity and enhancing broader public access. (Caswell et al., 2011: 1)

"Unearthing St. Augustine" led to the development and submission of another NEH proposal titled "Exploring Historic St. Augustine: Mobile Humanities Tours for the Nation's Oldest City."

In 2015 the nation celebrates the 450th anniversary of the founding of St. Augustine in 1565. Popularly called "The Oldest City," this town of 14,000 people has survived longer, and preserved more of its original layout, than any other city in the 50 states. It is rivaled only by the pueblo towns of the Southwest and San Juan, Puerto Rico, in overall longevity. Although many of the educational activities and outreach programming will be oriented towards this historic anniversary, UF and its partners intend to establish an ongoing program that will endure beyond the celebration next year.

This ambitious public programming project will use humanities resources to engage and educate general audiences (both onsite and virtually) to St. Augustine's many historical, cultural, architectural and archeological treasures. The project will develop and promote: 1) An *Exploring Historic St. Augustine* website (using responsive web design) featuring interpretive and educational tours of the city. 2) Two kiosks in the main lobby of Government House historic site in St. Augustine featuring iPad tablets delivering the *Exploring Historic St. Augustine* website. 3) A portable kiosk for temporary use in venues such as the St. Augustine Visitor Information Center, the UF campus in Gainesville, or at conferences and special events around the state and nation. (Caswell et al., 2014: 7)

"Exploring Historic St. Augustine" could not have been conceived without the preceding grant awards that laid the groundwork for collaborative relationships, digital content creation, and georeferencing software required to develop this new public tours initiative. Planning discussions during the "Exploring Historic St. Augustine" NEH proposal preparation phase contributed to strengthening relationships beyond the Florida Humanities Council staff, members of the Historic St. Augustine Research Institute, and members of the St. Augustine Historical Society. Although the NEH Public Programs review panel declined the "Exploring Historic St. Augustine" application, the creation of a mobile app component of this project materialized through funding from the State of Florida to the Florida Humanities Council (FHC), which is leading the effort, while UF Libraries' staff continue to fully support the new FHC app project by providing the necessary historical resources to fulfill its content requirements.

To see the project result, download FHC's new Florida Stories app: https://itunes.apple.com/us/app/id1012015225 (for the Apple version) or https://play.google.com/store/apps/details?id=com.flahum (for the Android version). More information and audio links to stories of St. Augustine can be found at http://www.flstories.org.

Subsequently, the description of the proposed public humanities position presented in the "Exploring Historic St. Augustine" proposal was used successfully to advocate for the establishment of this position (digital preservation curator), funded through a partnership between the Smathers Libraries and the UF Historic St. Augustine Inc.

National Competition for Expanding Artists' Book Collection

"Creating a National Juried Selection Process for an Artists' Book Collection" was the Mini Grant invention of book artist and curator of book arts Ellen Knudson in 2010. Knudson had just joined the Smathers Libraries in this new position and realized the lack of exemplary works produced by student book artists in the collection. Her Mini Grant proposal noted that the Libraries have

a very strong sampling of book arts publications in the areas of Fine Press, Typography and Printing History. . . . There is a desire within the Special Collections library, the School of Art and Art History and the Department of English, to have physical access to high quality artists' books currently being produced in the U.S. This proposal requests funds [$4,883] for acquiring artists' books created by graduate students in book arts programs in the U.S. through a Call for Submissions, an exhibition of the work, purchase, and placement of the work in the libraries' permanent collection. . . .

The exhibition of contemporary artists' books created by graduate students in national book arts programs will invigorate the libraries and introduce UF students to a broad range of books being produced by peer artists.... The importance and use of seeing work done by peers, in addition to seasoned artists, is the recognition that the goal of creating distinctive work is attainable. ... When being introduced to a new medium, it is inspirational to touch and interact with work produced by contemporaries in conjunction with more complex, master work. (Knudson and de Farber, 2009: 1–2)

To support the program beyond its initial Mini Grant award, funds from an endowment were identified as a good match in satisfying the donor's wishes for use of endowment income. Since 2009, the annual competition has proven to be wholly original in the state of Florida, and also may be unique in the United States. It has created a high-quality collection of ninety-six original works, generated online exhibits, and fostered collaborative relationships with faculty and students from Flagler College in St. Augustine, which hosted an ARTBOUND traveling exhibit in 2015. In 2014, UF student works were among those selected for inclusion in the collection, thus validating the original intent of the application request.

Librarian-Mediated Literature Searches

The Health Science Center Library (HSCL) liaison librarian, Jenner Lyon, generated a project in 2010 titled "Analyzing Librarian-Mediated Literature Searches in the Health Sciences" to test an alternative use of REDCap, a database system traditionally used to analyze clinical research data. The proposed project goal was to

> record and examine the mediated searches that HSCL librarians conduct for their patrons.... HSCL took advantage of having free access to a clinical trial data management system, REDCap, to develop an electronic database to store librarian conducted searches. Prior to this [proposal], there was no established procedure to digitally record and analyze complex literature searches and mediated results. Additionally, as far as can be ascertained, no one has used the REDCap system for this purpose.... The advantage of REDCap for this type of project is that it allows rapid form development, control of user rights, ability to protect confidential data, easy data entry, reporting and analysis, and ability to feed specified data selections to other software tools and user interfaces.... The Biomedical and Health Information Services department has over 800 paper requests for literature searches from 2004–2010 stored in a cabinet and that data is not convenient for reuse or evaluation unless it is transferred into electronic form. Therefore, we are seeking funding to hire student workers to enter the past data into our new database so that it is amenable to analysis and comparison with present and future data. (Lyon, 2010: 3)

As of this publication, the team continues to use the system for this purpose and now REDCap tracks reference statistics as well. A subsequent article published in *Medical Reference Services Quarterly* indicated that "having search data readily available allows librarians to reuse search strategies and track their workload. In aggregate, this data can help guide practice and determine priorities by identifying users' needs, tracking librarian effort and focusing librarians' continuing education" (Lyon et al., 2014: 241).

The far-reaching outcomes of the Library Mediated Literature Searches Mini Grant project demonstrate the potential results that can be generated by a relatively small award of $1,688. That project yielded other unexpected benefits as described in the Ian Parker Collection of Elephant Data.

Ian Parker Collection of Elephant Data

In 2013, African studies librarian and anthropologist Dan Reboussin, PhD, was planning a Mini Grant project to transcribe and electronically capture data held within manuscript records, part of the Ian Parker Collection of East African Wildlife Conservation, produced after the culling of elephant families in east Africa, "to mitigate elephant overpopulation at environmentally stressed sites from 1965 to 1969" (Reboussin and Norton, 2013: 2). Unlike print sources, simply digitizing these manuscripts would not be helpful to researchers. "Manuscript records, in contrast, are not candidates for reliable OCR (Optical Character Recognition) analysis. Historical scientific data projects often opt for manual transcription to assure accurate results from handwriting" (Reboussin and Norton, 2013: 2).

Based on the success of the 2010–2011 HSCL Librarian-Mediated Literature Searches project, the idea of using REDCap for another Mini Grant proposal to transcribe a much larger collection was submitted. Manuscript pages from the Parker Collection contained data related to

> body and organ measurements, age estimates, reproductive status, and disease observations . . . collected post mortem and recorded on 3,175 data sheets. . . . The Elephant Data Sheets are unique in several ways: the large number of individuals is unlikely to be reproduced; the sampling represents natural (albeit environmentally stressed) family groups rather than trophics or weak individuals; and until now the records have been unavailable to the public. (Reboussin and Norton, 2013: 3)

The award of $5,000 was used to temporarily hire seven students who were trained to enter the transcription data, much of which was difficult to read, contained various types of measuring methods, and posed numerous challenges. In exploring the various benefits that a library project like this one could have, Reboussin shared his anticipated outcomes:

> The . . . endorsement letters . . . indicate that [the dataset] will attract interest and recognition across diverse disciplines. Providing convenient, state of the art, fully open access to these data will create new educational and research opportunities in support of academic programs such as wildlife conservation, mammalian biology, and zoo and wildlife veterinary medicine in at least four major STEM units on the UF campus: the Colleges of Agricultural and Life Sciences, Liberal Arts and Sciences, and Veterinary Medicine, along with the Florida Museum of Natural History. Direct, convenient, online access to this newly available, unique, empirical data source will encourage analyses that were not considered in the original publication (Laws et al. 1975) and create an opportunity for reanalysis of the published data. (Reboussin and Norton, 2013: 3)

And in terms of direct impact on the Smathers Libraries, Reboussin continues to make his case:

> The data sheets project will encourage the development of data curation supports both during and after the grant period, provoking institutional learning to plan and provide appropriate support for the curation and preservation of more and larger data sets in libraries. As an example, these data and their associated image files in UFDC [UF Digital Collections] offer a real world test bed for the development of a database module in SOBEK/CM (Sullivan, 2013), with potential features such as guided queries, display of results in clusters that may be examined together, and the mapping of linked case numbers by location as recorded on the sheets. (Reboussin and Norton, 2013: 3)

The transcription and digitization of the Parker elephant data sheets and related materials in the UF Digital Collections demonstrated the Libraries' active promotion of Parker's collection for research access. This collection, combined with previously donated African wildlife conservation collections at UF, formed the basis of a significant cluster of research materials. Increased public access to these freely available resources has at this writing attracted two additional major collection gifts. The first is Alistair Graham's survey data and maps documenting crocodile populations in Kenya, Botswana, Uganda, and Ethiopia. The most recent donation of African wildlife–related materials is from photographer Bob Campbell, whose photographic slides and diaries document Dian Fossey's work with mountain gorillas at Mount Karisoke in Rwanda. His images in *National Geographic* and in Fossey's 1983 book, *Gorillas in the Mist* (released as an Academy Award–winning movie in 1983), can be expected to broaden interest in this large and unique research cluster of African wildlife conservation materials that UF has built over the past five years.

Digitizing Jewish Newspapers for Preservation and Access

The curator of the Price Library of Judaica at the Smathers Libraries, Rebecca Jefferson, PhD, accepted this position at UF in 2010 while working at the University of Cambridge, England. Upon her arrival, her predecessor forewarned her about the poor state of preservation of a collection of anniversary newspapers from all over the world. Jefferson recognized the enormous value of this entirely hidden collection. Her first ever grant application, a Mini Grant proposal ($2,390 award) thus focused on digitizing and producing original cataloging records for thirty-two of the anniversary issues. These editions were published in nineteen different cities of the world with major Jewish populations. The resulting interest of over 1,800 online, unique visitors to this obscure collection inspired Jefferson to seek additional Mini Grant funds ($1,280) for the project titled "Moving Forward!—A Second-Phase Project to Digitize Anniversary Issues of the Legendary American Jewish Newspaper the *Forverts* (*Jewish Daily Forward*): A Special Sub-collection within the Price Library of Judaica Anniversary Collection." The project digitized twenty-two anniversary issues, from 1917 to 1967, that were deteriorating rapidly, and upon project completion coincided with the *Forverts*' 115th anniversary year.

> The Forverts is a highly significant newspaper due to its longevity (1897 to present day), its world renown and for the regard in which it is held by Jewish people as a much beloved Jewish institution. . . . At the height of its popularity in the 1930s, the Forverts was one of America's premier dailies with a circulation of 275,000. The Forverts not only addressed the key issues of the day, it also featured literary giants, like Isaac Bashevis Singer and [Elie] Wiesel and introduced the Jewish reading public to new Jewish artists. . . . Indeed, the Forverts was unique as a foreign language newspaper [Yiddish] that actually aided the Americanization of immigrants. (Jefferson and de Farber, 2011: 1)

This collection became one of the Price Library's top visited online titles. Jefferson soon realized that exposing hidden digital newspapers online broadened the awareness of the Price Library's existence and attracted the greatest interest. Having these two successful experiences prompted Jefferson to work with the Libraries' grants manager to apply for the state of Florida's Library Services and Technology Act grant funds. The application, titled "Florida Digital Newspaper Library: Broadening Access and Users," received $21,753 "to provide technical assistance and training to broaden access to the

Florida Digital Newspaper Library [FDNL] and highlight 'hidden' local and ethnic Florida newspapers" (Jefferson and de Farber 2012a: 3), specifically the *Jewish Floridian* (1928–1990). At the time of application, anyone interested in viewing this "hidden" newspaper had to travel to UF or to the Jewish Museum of Florida in Miami Beach for access to the two available microfilm collections. Beyond exposing the newspaper online (which at the time of this writing had received 4,700 visitors totaling 1.8 million views), the project team created a webinar promoted throughout Dade, Broward, and Martin Counties (counties with the largest percentage of Jewish residents in Florida) and an accompanying tutorial, highlighting the *Jewish Floridian* and other Florida ethnic newspapers in the FDNL collections, as a means for assisting those who wanted to know best practices for searching any newspaper in the FDNL (there are currently 187,795 pages in this growing collection).

Promoting a Collection through Live Performance

Another interesting Mini Grant submitted by Jefferson in 2012, titled "A Performing Arts Approach to Collection Development," was awarded $3,769, as a proof-of-concept for potential external funding. This project explored the use of live dramatic performances—depicting stories of immigrant journeys held within the Price Library collections—and the resulting impacts on audiences (Jefferson and de Farber, 2012b). Jefferson had previously cosponsored a performance of *Composing a Heart*, for clarinet, storyteller, and multimedia, about the immigrant lives of married cousins from Bielsk, Poland, and Buenos Aires, Argentina, who settled in Miami, Florida. Positive audience feedback and a subsequent book donation to the Price Library by an enthusiastic audience member prompted Jefferson to find stories in the collection that might promote the collection to broader audiences while inspiring more contributions.

To experiment with this innovative concept, Kevin Marshall, director of theatre and the Center for the Arts and Public Policy at UF, agreed to plan and present three multimedia performances of stories from the collection, and Sophia Accord, assistant director for the Center for the Humanities and the Public Sphere, joined the project team as project evaluator. Two stories were selected: Leah Stupniker, a fourteen-year-old girl whose family sailed to Ellis Island from Palestine and who died of tuberculosis just days before reaching the United States; and Emanuel Merdinger, professor of chemistry at UF, who survived Nazi persecution in Romania by making beer for German troops.

The performance, *A Handful of Leaves*, premiered at the Digital Worlds Institute at UF in 2013. Interviews with audience members and student actors noted the many positive and personal benefits the performances produced. Beyond exposing the Price Library to over three hundred new potential supporters, this unusual collaborative project resulted in donations to UF and presentations at the Qualitative Report Conference, the Imagining America Conference, and Arts in Society International Conference in Budapest. Marshall completed another premiere, *Gator Tales*, a theatrical presentation of stories held in the Samuel Proctor Oral History Program collections at UF. These stories recount the experiences of UF alumni during the civil rights movement of the 1960s—presenting hidden stories and voices of dramatic events that occurred in Gainesville, Florida. The world premiere of *Gator Tales* was presented at the 2015 Fringe Festival in Edinburgh, Scotland.

The "performing arts approach" also was included in the subsequent NEH Challenge Grant application titled "Repositioning Florida's Judaica Library: Increasing Access to Humanities Resources from Florida, Latin America, and the Caribbean Communities."

This project leverages previously awarded projects that established the Digital Library of the Caribbean hosted by UF (Jefferson et al., 2014). The awarded Challenge Grant provides $500,000 from NEH—for each $3 in new funding raised for the project, NEH will provide $1 in federal matching funds. A modified performance, *Composing a Heart and Other Jewish Immigrant Stories*, is providing a means for exposing Price Library holdings to potential donor audiences and motivating new contributions to the library.

⊚ Key Points

Librarians and library staff members who are interested in learning to prepare fundable grant proposals can benefit greatly from participating in an internally funded grantmaking program. These are some important recommendations to consider when creating a mini-grant program:

- The grants committee should include representatives from throughout the library's operations.
- A budget line for allocating mini-grant awards should have a designated annual source of funding.
- Mini-grant guidelines work best as training tools when they mirror the components and criteria of externally sponsored programs and guidelines.
- Working with a library's accounting staff at the beginning of planning a grant proposal can prevent unforeseen challenges.
- Coaching project directors and teams during the proposal development process leads to fundable projects and creates environments that support grant-seekers.

The next chapter presents strategies for collaboratively searching, documenting, and promoting external grant opportunities for libraries.

⊚ Appendix 3.1: Sample Mini-Grant Program Guidelines

The Library *Mini Grant Program* is open to all staff from the George Smathers Libraries. This program has been designed to provide a supportive environment for those who wish to gain experience conceptualizing, writing, and administering grant projects. Successful grant projects are competitively selected and are funded and administered by the University of Florida Libraries Grant Management Committee. The Mini Grant Program is intended to replicate, as much as possible, the process of writing and submitting grant proposals to outside funding agencies. Guidelines, application and FAQs for this program are available on the Funding Opportunities Guide (http://guides.uflib.ufl.edu/funding), under the Mini Grant Program for Library Faculty and Staff tab.

Deadlines: May 15, 2013 and October 15, 2014

Contact Person: Bess de Farber, Grants Manager, (425 Library West; bdefarber@ufl.edu or 273-2519) or any member of the Grants Management Committee. The Grants Management Committee encourages you to contact Bess for assistance in developing your project idea, proposal, and budget.

Application Requirements

1. The Mini Grant Program is an annual library grant writing competition. It offers funding for creative and innovative programs and services that enhance and support the mission (http://www.uflib.ufl.edu/staff-site/goals/directions.html) and goals (http://www.uflib.ufl.edu/staff-site/goals/goals.html) of the Smathers Libraries. All proposal submissions will be reviewed and scored by a judging panel. Proposals endorsed by the Grants Management Committee will be reviewed by the Dean of Libraries, who will ultimately determine if funding is approved. To create a strong proposal, applicants should closely follow the requirements stated here and should familiarize themselves with the "Judging Criteria" included below. Applicants may also wish to browse awarded submissions from prior grant cycles, available on the **Mini Grant Program for Library Faculty and Staff** tab.

2. Rules of eligibility: This competition is open to all library staff (except OPS). Preference will be given to proposals from applicants who have limited grant writing experience. Please note: individuals, regardless of previous grant-writing experience, or those who have previously received a Mini Grant award as a principal investigator on a project are eligible to be the PI on future Mini Grant applications.

3. Awards will have a maximum dollar limit of $5,000.

4. The duration of the award period is a maximum of 12 months from date of award.

5. Please follow instructions on the cover sheet and application form for use of library resources.

6. Collaboration on mini grant proposals is required. However, one person must be designated as the principal investigator (PI) for the grant. There is a 10% cost share requirement for the Mini Grant Program, towards which the lead PI on a project *cannot* contribute their own salaried time. However, the budget must include an estimate of the cost share effort the PI plans to contribute thus providing review committee members a more complete picture of the project.

7. There will be no indirect cost (overhead expenses) obligation.

8. Proposals with strong letters/email messages of commitment and support are more likely to be awarded than those without. Applicants are encouraged to ask other librarians, researchers, or teaching faculty to write in support of their proposed project.

9. As with all external proposals, applicants are required to work in partnership with the Library Grants Manager prior to submission.

10. For digitization projects, please see the guidelines for budgets and submission to the Internet Archive.

List of Required Documents for Application

1. Cover sheet with signatures and initials
2. Project Proposal Narrative and Budget Narrative (5 pages)
3. Budget Form for all proposal related expenses
4. Appendix A: Letters or email messages of support (maximum 3) from those who support the project and can validate its importance to scholarship, preservation, accessibility, or in other ways to benefit UF.

5. Appendix B: Letters or email messages of commitment—some collaborative projects and those that serve more than one professor on campus, require additional letters to confirm participation outlined in the narrative, or adopt and use the project product.

NOTE: Additional appendices as needed, however please note that the narrative cannot be substituted by appendices.

Application Submission Procedure

Email electronic copies of all documents to Bess de Farber. Please provide a scanned copy of the coversheet with signatures.

Judging Criteria

The judging panel will consist of the membership of the Grants Management Committee. Each proposal will be evaluated according to the same criteria:

1. The proposal's support for library professional activities that enhance access to and academic use of information, or that support the instructional, research and public service endeavors of the libraries and the university; and, the degree to which the proposal justifies a specific need for the project.
2. The presentation and completeness of the proposal and how well the budget request matches with specific activities proposed (including costs for equipment, supplies, personnel, etc.).
3. The potential for long-term benefit to the library and university (including the potential to attract additional funding), such as: new directions of investigation, enhancement of services and activities, improved access to information, or professional development.
4. The degree to which the proposed project is innovative in terms of being the first or one of the first such projects in the country. Emphasis will be given to evidence which compares the proposed project to other similar projects at other academic libraries.

For projects intended to continue beyond the 12-month scope of the Mini Grant, applicants should explain to the review panel how the project will be sustained after grant funds are expended. Applicants may wish to frame their proposals as "seed grant" proposals—projects with a limited scope, worthwhile in themselves, that also have the potential to attract more funding or to develop into major projects.

In cases where applicants are requesting travel funds, they should first investigate whether these funds can be obtained as part of official library business or as part of the library's development initiative. Grant budgets should include travel expenses only if the travel is an essential part of a project and cannot be funded by other means.

Approval Process

Each proposal is reviewed by members of the Grants Management Committee (GMC) based on criteria listed above. Members will develop a list of questions for applicants to clarify shortly after submission. The GMC Chair and Library Grants Manager will meet with applicants to review questions and obtain responses that will then inform GMC's funding recommendations to the Dean of the Libraries, who makes the final determination of awards and declinations.

Deadlines and Schedules

Spring Cycle: 2013–2014 Mini Grant Deadlines

- Applications are due to Bess de Farber, in the grants office, LW 425, or they can be sent electronically to besdefa@uflib.ufl.edu by 5:00PM, Wednesday, May 15, 2013. The Grants Management Committee will review proposals in late May and June.
- Notification of awards and release of funds will be made by the end of June for a grant starting date of July 1, 2013.
- All grant projects receiving awards must expend awarded funds by June 30, 2014 and the projects must be completed by and final reports due on July 31, 2014.

Fall Cycle: 2013–2014 Mini Grant Deadlines

- Applications are due to Bess de Farber, in the grants office, LW 425, or they can be sent electronically to besdefa@uflib.ufl.edu by 5:00PM, October 15, 2013. The Grants Management Committee will review proposals shortly thereafter.
- Notification of awards and release of funds will be made by mid-November for a grant period starting date of November 15, 2013.
- All grant projects receiving awards must expend awarded funds by November 14, 2014 and the projects must be completed by and final reports due on December 15, 2014.

References

Caswell, Thomas. 2008. "Historic St. Augustine Block and Lot Files Digitization." The Institutional Repository at the University of Florida. October 1. http://ufdc.ufl.edu/UF00091743/00001.

Caswell, Thomas, James Cusick, John Nemmers, and Bess de Farber. 2011. "Unearthing St. Augustine's Colonial Heritage: An Interactive Digital Collection for the Nation's Oldest City." The Institutional Repository at the University of Florida. July 20. http://ufdc.ufl.edu/AA00004298/00001.

Caswell, Thomas, James Cusick, John Nemmers, Elizabeth Haven Hawley, and Bess de Farber. 2014. "Exploring St. Augustine: Mobile Humanities Tours for the Nation's Oldest City." The Institutional Repository at the University of Florida. August 13. http://ufdc.ufl.edu/AA00025533/00001.

Conlon, Michael. 2009. "VIVO: Enabling National Networking of Scientists." The Institutional Repository at the University of Florida. June 26. http://ufdc.ufl.edu/UF00094181/00001.

Getz, Kelli, Miranda Henry Bennett, and Nancy Linden. 2014. "Encouraging Entrepreneurism with Internal Small Grants: The Strategic Directions Microgrant Program at the University of Houston Libraries." *Journal of Library Innovation* 1, no. 5: 55–66.

Jefferson, Rebecca, and Bess de Farber. 2010. "The Price Library of Judaica Anniversary Collection: A First Project to Digitize a Unique Set of Jewish Newspapers." The Institutional Repository at the University of Florida. October 13. http://ufdc.ufl.edu/UF00103161/00001.

———. 2011. "Moving Forward! A Second-Phase Project to Digitize Anniversary Issues of the Legendary American Jewish Newspaper, the *Forverts* (*Jewish Daily Forward*): A Special Sub-collection within the Price Library of Judaica Anniversary Collection." The Institutional Repository at the University of Florida. October 3. http://ufdc.ufl.edu/IR00000778/00001.

———. 2012a. "The Florida Digital Newspaper Library: Broadening Access and Users." The Institutional Repository at the University of Florida. March 16. http://ufdc.ufl.edu/AA00010438/00001.

———. 2012b. "A Performing Arts Approach to Collection Development." The Institutional Repository at the University of Florida. October 15. http://ufdc.ufl.edu/AA00013460/00001.

Jefferson, Rebecca, Bess de Farber, John Nemmers, et al. 2014. "Repositioning Florida's Judaica Library: Increasing Access to Humanities Resources from Florida, Latin America, and the Caribbean Communities." The Institutional Repository at the University of Florida. http://ufdc.ufl.edu/AA00022790/00001.

Knudson, Ellen, and Bess de Farber. 2009. "Creating an Interdisciplinary Artists' Book Collection for Smathers and Architecture/Fine Arts Libraries." The Institutional Repository at the University of Florida. October 1. http://ufdc.ufl.edu/IR00000190/00001.

Lyon, Jennifer A. 2010. "Analyzing Librarian-Mediated Literature Searches in the Health Sciences." The Institutional Repository at the University of Florida. October 12. http://ufdc.ufl.edu/UF00103191/00001.

Lyon, Jennifer A., Rolando Garcia-Milian, Hannah F. Norton, and Michele R. Tennant. 2014. "The Use of Research Electronic Data Capture (REDCap) Software to Create a Database of Librarian-Mediated Literature Searches." *Medical Reference Services Quarterly* 33, no. 3 (July–September): 241–52. http://dx.doi.org/10.1080/02763869.2014.925379.

Minson, Valrie, and Sara Russell Gonzalez. 2007. "GatorScholar: Developing a Database to Foster Interdisciplinary Communication and Collaboration at UF." The Institutional Repository at the University of Florida. October 1. http://ufdc.ufl.edu/UF00091758/00001.

Reboussin, Daniel, and Hannah Norton. 2013. "The Parker Elephant Data Sheets: A Library Mini-grant Project Proposal." The Institutional Repository at the University of Florida. May 1. http://ufdc.ufl.edu/IR00003175/00001.

CHAPTER 4

Searching for External Grant Opportunities

THIS CHAPTER PROVIDES THE BASIC information and resources necessary to identify funding opportunities for which librarians and libraries can apply. With the establishment of a mini-grant program, librarians are prepared to undertake methods that increase their awareness of external funding opportunities and knowledge about how to apply for specific opportunities. Either a grants coordinator or members of a grants management committee themselves can lead these efforts. As well, some librarians may be inclined to voluntarily assist, from time to time, with certain tasks that fall naturally within their expertise.

Identifying grant opportunities on a regular basis is the framework necessary for establishing a functioning library grants program. As library personnel increase their knowledge and understanding of available resources, they will become empowered and positioned to generate ongoing interest and participation in grant-seeking activities over time. It is important to remember that searching for grant opportunities should never stop; rather, searching activities should become part of a library's essential, expected routine.

Continuously searching for grant opportunities that are appropriate for librarians and/or libraries is a threshold requirement for growing a culture of grantsmanship. Finding opportunities that match up with a librarian's projects or interests can be an effective way of fueling continued participation in the grant-seeking process. In general, making librarians continuously informed about available and appropriate funding opportunities is one of the key ways to grow a successful program. Fortunately, librarians invariably demonstrate an abiding aptitude and natural curiosity for seeking out information. Searching for grant opportunities, however, may be new to many.

Librarians would be well advised to look for grant opportunities that are of immediate interest to any librarians or staff in the library as well as opportunities that might fit nicely into future plans. Pooling the efforts of librarians to work as a team is an excellent strategy for finding these opportunities. Identifying a small cadre of librarians who are initially interested in searching for grant opportunities is a good method for both focusing and at the same time sharing the workload and introducing a collaborative searching approach. This affinity group can essentially work together while learning and exploring possibilities. Once the group has practiced using various online databases, search engines, and news sources, then they can become experts for training others on how to navigate for the most optimal results. Combining forces to carry on the searching process, month after month, will produce many more opportunities than might be immediately necessary. With practice, librarians will become increasingly educated about sources of funding, the types of projects sponsors are seeking, and the deadlines that drive planning and preparation timelines.

A review of some basic characteristics of the types of sponsors that support libraries and their programs, projects, research, and facilities will provide the context for future discussion of the options and steps for searching.

Government (Public) Grant Opportunities

Government grant sponsors are excellent sources of funding for libraries. These sponsors have long-term commitments to the library field on local, state, and national levels. Government funding programs normally employ staff members dedicated to providing technical assistance, training, and guidance for potential applicants. Because these agencies have missions grounded in providing service and assistance, their staff members are very helpful and supportive. Websites generally present information about government funding, often containing clear funding guidelines (also referred to as solicitations), examples of previously funded applications, full disclosures of awardees with accompanying grant amounts, and abstracts summarizing funded proposals. They often provide in-depth descriptions of programs with specific deadlines.

Government sponsors sometimes offer training workshops on grant opportunities. They are most predictable in disclosing information in a timely fashion and in maintaining a consistent array of program areas with few changes from year to year. These sponsors also may fund programs beyond one year and with major award allocations, although awards come with restrictions on the use of funds and with extensive reporting requirements.

The Institute of Museum and Library Services (IMLS) is the nation's sponsor dedicated to supporting libraries and museums. Its funds support a variety of activities and research based on strategic goals adopted every few years through its national planning process. Further, IMLS administers funding allocations to each state pursuant to the Library Services and Technology Act (LSTA). This source is the largest federal program exclusively funding library services with over $150 million allocated annually. Funds are distributed through state archives and libraries based on population (IMLS, 2015).

Other government programs also function to fund libraries as well as other types of organizations, either annually or as one-time opportunities. These programs primarily do not restrict eligibility to just one type of organization such as libraries, but rather focus on the types of projects, services, research, or facilities that best support the sponsor's mission and strategic goals.

On a local level, a city, county, or multiple-county region may sponsor several types of grants programs that are appropriate to libraries. Tourist development funds may be available through grants that are administered by a local arts agency or county tourist development council. A library program or project may be eligible for these funds that commonly support events, conferences, exhibitions, or performances. Funds administered by city or county parks and recreation departments are sometimes granted to promote public events.

Community redevelopment funds (federal funds administered by a local community redevelopment agency—CRA) may be offered for expanding or renovating library facilities or other activities depending on the individual CRA's grantmaking objectives. For instance, the CRA in Delray Beach, Florida, awarded grant funds for capital costs related to building a new Delray Beach Public Library facility ($1 million), and operational funding ($2,388,000) totaling $3,388,000 in awarded funds from 2002 to 2015.

Beyond the LSTA grant programs, state libraries, or archives, other potential state sponsors for funding librarians or libraries include departments or offices focused on historical preservation, statewide arts and cultural affairs, economic development, public health, social services, or the environment. It is easy to imagine how librarians can participate in these areas of service for improving their communities or benefiting their constituents. The point here is that in terms of local and state government support, librarians should be well versed in what funding opportunities are potentially available—and the agencies that administer these grantmaking processes—to support community projects or programs. Some of these opportunities may be perfect matches for supporting a library's endeavors.

Using the online search language "state of [fill in your state] funding for nonprofits" will yield sites—usually including the state's department of budget and management—containing lists of available grant deadlines with brief descriptions of the sponsor's funding programs. You might also search for nonprofit agencies or libraries within the state that have received grant funds and work backward to locate the appropriate funding opportunity description (also called request for proposal or RFP) for which a grant was awarded, along with the sponsor's identity.

In addition to IMLS, other possible national sponsors with applicable programs for libraries include the National Historic Publications and Records Commission (http://www.archives.gov/nhprc/announcement/); National Science Foundation (http://www.nsf.gov/funding/); National Institutes of Health (NIH) (http://grants.nih.gov/grants/oer.htm); and the National Network of Libraries of Medicine (NN/LM) (https://nnlm.gov/). As part of the NIH, the National Library of Medicine (http://www.nlm.nih.gov/grants.html) provides grants to organizations and fellowships to individuals. The grants.gov website (http://www.grants.gov), provides the most current information about federal government funding opportunities and related deadlines. All librarians should be familiar with the information provided on this site because regardless of the opportunity, all federal agency grant applications must be uploaded using the grants.gov submission system.

Due largely to the increased accessibility of information related to deadlines and funding opportunities, government agencies have been receiving many more applications in recent years. Reductions in funding allocations, especially to humanities, historical preservation, and arts-focused programs, have compounded the issue of increased competition. This combination has stretched federal agency staff members, who also have suffered staff reductions and consolidations of departments. Nonetheless, they continue to innovate guidelines and add new programs. For instance, IMLS is experimenting with guidelines that request two-page letters of intent as initial submissions to determine which applicants will be invited to submit full proposals for a second round of reviews. Paying attention to changes in guidelines for programs that routinely award grants to libraries will further enable librarians to become increasingly knowledgeable about the world of government grant opportunities and agency protocols.

Foundation Grant Opportunities

Foundations vary widely in staff size, proximity to applicants, program foci, and size of awards. Grant awards from foundations are generally smaller than government sponsors, and they are usually for one-year grant periods. Review processes, application formats, and application review schedules may or may not be formalized. Foundations are more likely than government sponsors to invest in new projects without prerequisite plans or assessments. Most have policies for benefiting specific communities of interest to their trustees. The review process is generally shorter than that of government sponsors. Foundations employ fewer employees and sometimes operate without paid staff, thus limiting the amount of assistance provided to potential applicants. This allows for the best use of private dollars for benefiting and improving communities.

There are several types of foundations, legally defined as such by the U.S. tax code. According to the Foundation Center's *Foundations Today Tutorial*, foundations are nonprofit organizations managed by appointed trustees and directors, with missions primarily to support the activities operated by other charitable programs for the public good, and which make grants to nonprofit organizations and individuals. Private foundations can be categorized as independent or family foundations; company-sponsored or corporate foundations; or operating foundations. Independent or family foundations manage endowment funds contributed by a small number of individual donors or family members (IRS, 2014: 1). Kerry Hannon of the *New York Times* writes that "there are now over 40,000 family foundations in the United States, making grants totaling more than $21.3 billion a year, up from about 3,200 family foundations doling out $6.8 billion in 2001, according to the Foundation Center in Washington" (Hannon, 2014). The Gates Family Foundation is a premier example of a family foundation. Others among the top ten grantors (based on annual giving) include the John D. and Catherine T. MacArthur Foundation, Ford Foundation, Robert Wood Johnson Foundation, and the W. K. Kellogg Foundation (Foundation Center, 2015f).

Company-sponsored corporate foundations manage funds received from parent companies and operate as entities separate from the founding company. Some corporate foundations include the Wells Fargo Foundation, the Wal-Mart Foundation, the Bank of

America Charitable Foundation Inc., and GE Foundation (ranked in the top ten foundations nationally) (Foundation Center, 2015e).

According to the Council on Foundations (2015), there are two types of organizations classified as 501(c)(3) tax-exempt charitable organizations: public charities and private foundations (http://www.cof.org/content/foundation-basics). A distinction can be made between grantmaking foundations (also called private nonoperating foundations), and private operating foundations, which receive funding from a limited number of contributors and are not in the business of awarding grants to outside organizations. Instead, these organizations allocate funds to support in-house programs and research (Foundation Center, 2015b).

Public foundations, also called grantmaking public charities, are those that continuously seek and accept funds from the general public and a wide variety of sources. Grantmaking to nonprofit organizations is a primary mission of these types of foundations. Grant awards by public foundations are made to various nonprofit organizations based on stated priorities of the foundation that are outlined in funding guidelines. This type of foundation includes community foundations and United Way organizations.

Recently, the women's funding movement has popularized the growing field of women's funds, which raise funds and make grants to empower women and girls and their causes. At the time of this writing, there are 160 funds and foundations in thirty countries that are part of the Women's Funding Network (Women's Funding Network, 2015).

It should be noted that there is a plethora of organizations for which the word "foundation" is included within the organization's name. Not all of these organizations, however, award grant funds. Many of these organizations have simply adopted the term as a means for communicating charitable intent. The University of Florida Foundation is not classified as a foundation by the IRS; it is simply a 501(c)(3) charitable organization. The reverse also is possible. An organization may function as a grantmaking foundation but may exclude the word "foundation" from its title. The IRS has no requirement or policy in terms of including or excluding "foundation" from an organization's name (Walsh, 2015).

Nonprofit Charitable Organizations

Discerning whether or not an organization is in the grantmaking business can be tricky. In addition to other functions, some nonprofit charitable organizations also award grant funds. Many organizations that are not government agencies, for instance, make grants to applicant organizations by using government "pass-through" grant funds. An example is the National Network of Libraries of Medicine, which is a membership-based organization coordinated by the National Library of Medicine. Its funding to public and academic libraries comes from NIH. Local arts agencies are another example. These agencies are generally membership-based support service organizations that are often private nonprofit 501(c)(3) IRS-designated charitable organizations—some of which are public/private partnerships, meaning that half or more of the agency's operating budget comes from government sources. Many local arts agencies are grantmakers that have agreements with local government agencies to distribute tax dollars through grant awards such as tourist development funds, public art funds, or outreach and promotional funds.

Other examples of membership-based organizations include the American Library Association, Council on Library and Information Resources, Center for Research Libraries, and humanities councils that can be found in every state. All are nonprofit organizations that also provide grant funding as a means of furthering their missions. Funding for grants may come from membership dues, and from programs sponsored by foundations, corporations, or government agencies.

To rephrase a cliché, you cannot always judge a book by its title. In the case of nongovernment sponsors, librarians should avoid making assumptions about whether a sponsor's funds are public or private. It is important to know the original source of the money being granted. Public versus private funding rules pertaining to allowable and disallowable expenses—and how funds must be managed—are different. Knowing this distinction can make a difference in how proposals are prepared and, if awarded, how the grant funds must be managed.

For instance, federal funds generally should not be budgeted for purchasing general supplies, computers, or food. This is because these types of expenses cannot accurately be tracked in terms of direct use for a funded project. Another example is illustrated by the situation in which federal funds are being regranted by a nonprofit organization to libraries, but because of a subcontract arrangement with a second party, the nonprofit sponsor is prohibited from allowing no-cost extensions (where the project team needs more time, not money, to finish the project). In the case of foundations, if the project has been completed successfully without spending all awarded grant funds, it is often the case that the foundation will allow the grantee organization to retain the remaining funds. Each situation is unique, depending on whether the type of funds is public or private.

There are ways to determine the full identity of an organization. For example, Guide-Star (http://www.guidestar.org), a free online service, provides information about charitable organizations. It is a good idea to subscribe to GuideStar as its resources are valuable to organizations in the business of fund-raising and/or grant-seeking. The home page contains a search box in which an organization name can be entered. If the search result fails to yield any records, the organization being searched is likely to have a different legal name, or is a government agency—not a nonprofit entity. Nonprofit organizations, which annually must submit IRS form 990 tax documents, including independent, family, operating, and public foundations, and all 501(c)(3) charitable organizations, will appear in the system. They also may employ a community relations professional to facilitate the library's request.

Corporate Sponsors

Funding from corporate sponsors—these are not foundations—can support a library's programs through cash donations or through in-kind contributions of goods and services. These sponsors also are an excellent source of volunteer labor for supporting special events or large coordinated activities. Corporate sponsors invariably seek public exposure and marketing opportunities in exchange for contributions. Those preparing proposals for corporate sponsors generally create what is commonly called a sponsorship package, which includes information about the marketing and promotional opportunities afforded the sponsor if the award is granted. Most corporations that are in the business of giving back to community organizations, such as Office Depot, Target, Starbucks, and Chipotle, provide simple online application forms for requesting contributions.

Eligibility of Libraries Primarily Supported by Public Funds

Sponsors generally include descriptions of eligibility requirements for potential applicants within their grant guidelines. Many foundations and corporations specify that eligible grant-seeking organizations must be designated by the IRS as nonprofit 501(c)(3) charitable organizations as specified in the organization's IRS letter of determination. The problem this presents is that most libraries are considered "public" because the majority of operating support comes from local or state government. These libraries may be ineligible to receive private funding, in many cases. There are exceptions when guidelines specify publicly supported entities as being eligible, so it is important to read the eligibility information provided by a prospective sponsor.

As a result, public libraries and academic libraries within public universities and colleges should be prepared to respond to such eligibility requirements. The first step is to confirm that applicants must be nonprofit organizations. If this provision is inflexible, then anyone seeking grant funds for a library project should ensure the applicant organization has the necessary IRS letter of determination. In the case of public academic institutions, the solution is to apply under the umbrella of the institution's sister organization that maintains this status. A university foundation is an example of an organization that serves this purpose. It has been established as a 501(c)(3) organization with the intent of raising funds from private donors, corporations, or foundations in support of the public university's colleges, departments, and libraries.

Public libraries may have a more challenging situation to resolve if they don't already have an established 501(c)(3) charitable library foundation or friends of the library organization whose mission is to seek and receive private support for its collections, programs, and services. There are tax advantages for those who contribute funds to 501(c)(3) charitable organizations, and as a result, these advantages can attract increased funding from a broad variety of donors, corporations, and private foundations that ultimately support public libraries, while also providing the necessary eligibility for grant-seeking. In Broward County, Florida, the Broward Public Library Foundation performs this role. According to the foundation's executive director, Dorothy Klein, as a 501(c)(3) charitable nonprofit organization (not a private foundation), it serves as the fiscal agent for grant applications prepared by the Broward County Public Library librarians and grant-writer, and works to raise funds from donors exclusively to support the public library's programs and projects.

⑥ Preparing to Search

Searching for library funding can be challenging. Beyond discerning the type of funding being granted, or the type of agency that is administering the grantmaking process, librarians who are searching for viable funding options can miss opportunities for other reasons. For instance, searching for sponsors that support libraries may be a good place to start, but this method has several limitations. Search results often yield funding information that is restricted to libraries located in a specific region of the country. The trick is in knowing that it is not necessarily about whether or not a sponsor funds libraries. It is more important to know what types of activities, program, projects, or results the potential sponsor has funded in the past and plans to fund in the future that may match up nicely with the librarian's project idea. Many sponsors fund libraries within their complement of awarded nonprofit organizations.

For instance, the Andrew W. Mellon Foundation funds art history, conservation, museums, performing arts, the humanities, scholarly communications and information technology, and specific types of organizations (Andrew W. Mellon Foundation, 2014). Funding to libraries may fit within these categories, especially proposals to support scholarly communications; but libraries are not explicitly identified.

Once a sponsor and its funding preferences are identified, the next step would be to view the awards granted in previous years. This can be achieved through searching the Foundation Directory Online, or at no cost at GuideStar. Reviewing the IRS form 990 will reveal a list of organizations supported and the amounts awarded for the time period applicable to the form. In the case of the Mellon Foundation, a better source is its Grants Database published in 2015, which allows for keyword searching of its grantmaking history (grantee, project title and short description, date of award, amount, and program category name) and features a map displaying the location of grantees. The foundation's annual report also provides valuable information about interests and giving priorities as well as a list of awardees and the amount and purpose of awards.

To prepare to search for funding opportunities of sponsors that only fund libraries and those that support nonprofit organizations of any type, you can benefit from knowing as much as possible about the library's assets, programs, and project ideas for which funding is desired or for which new opportunities for enhancements are known. Having access to this information makes searching much easier and rewarding. These questions may help generate responses that will be helpful:

- What specialized offerings may be unique to the library (services, collections, expertise, longevity of a specific program, facility design, etc.)?
- What activities or departments within the library have grown the most in the past two years?
- What unique types of populations are served by the library (single mothers, children who are part of free meal programs, veterans, the homeless, scholars searching for specific collection content)?
- What programs are particularly different and successful from those offered at other libraries?
- What types of new services or projects are of interest to librarians?
- What are the strategic directions outlined in the library's three-year plan that may require funding to actualize?

The answers to these questions will help inform the types of searches to perform. Librarians who begin searching with knowledge about the types of programs or projects that their library is developing or planning for the future are better prepared to spot opportunities they might have otherwise missed. This was the case during a workshop in 2011 at the University of Florida Libraries, which focused on training librarians to search for viable funding sources. A pair of librarians who were searching the National Science Foundation website came across the directorate for Ethics Education in Science and Engineering. After reading the guidelines for eligibility and the type of activities this program was seeking to fund, they realized that it matched up with work being performed by a few science librarians on the topic of plagiarism. Had they not known about this work, the librarians searching for funding opportunities would have missed the opportunity to share their find, and the science librarians would not have had the opportunity to apply and subsequently receive an award of $298,000 for the project titled "Gaming Against Plagiarism."

Where and How to Search

As mentioned previously, grants.gov is the site to locate deadlines for all federal agency–sponsored grant opportunities. It provides four options for searching: Newest Opportunities, Browse Categories, Browse Agencies, and Browse Eligibilities. Each subcategory within these tabs provides the number of grant opportunities in the subcategory (within parentheses). Grants.gov includes funding notifications from twenty-five agencies with over 1,700 grant opportunities at the time of this writing. The guidelines posted on federal agency sites are generally clear and understandable.

Other freely available sites featuring applicable deadlines include the following websites:

- Library Grants—http://www.scholastic.com/librarians/programs/grants.htm
- Funding for Libraries and Library Workers (University of Wisconsin, Madison, Libraries)—https://www.library.wisc.edu/memorial/collections/grants-information-collection/resources/funding for libraries-and-library-workers/
- Library Grants—http://librarygrants.blogspot.com/

Visiting a Foundation Center Library is another way to access free information. These libraries are sponsored by the Foundation Center and located in Atlanta, Cleveland, New York, San Francisco, and Washington, D.C. They provide trained staff and technical assistance in identifying prospective sponsors for specific programs or projects. Another service of the Foundation Center is its nationwide Funding Information Network with locations in libraries, community foundations, and nonprofit resource centers. These network partners also provide access to Internet and print resources that specialize in foundation and corporate giving programs. They also provide some assistance and training in searching for grantmaking organizations (Foundation Center, 2015c). A network partner is located in each state, and some regions offer multiple partners in various cities (Foundation Center, 2015a).

Databases available by subscription for searching grant opportunities offer multiple ways to find potential sponsors. The Foundation Directory Online provides information on private sponsors including over 120,000 private and corporate foundations, and grantmaking public charitable organizations. Many public libraries, and some academic libraries and foundations, provide access to this database. Five different subscription plans are offered, making this an affordable option for libraries. Another database is COS Pivot (http://pivot.cos.com) This is one of the largest providers of available funding opportunities for federal government agencies and foundation sponsors. COS encourages uploading profiles for exploring possible collaborative partners and features three million scholar profiles. Search results from COS can be overwhelmingly large, requiring considerable time to view many potential matches. GrantForward, formerly the University of Illinois Researcher Information Service (IRIS) (http://grantforward.com), is another resource for finding federal and private sponsors providing targeted search results. GrantSelect provides information on sponsors including federal and private sponsors, foundations, research institutes, state agencies, and universities (http://www.grantselect.com/index.html). The Chronicle of Philanthropy (http://philanthropy.com/section/Guide to Grants/270/) publishes a list of sponsors and deadlines in each publication and allows users to search grants, awards and prizes, products, and noncash support. It also features articles that provide insights into the world of giving. The textbox provides a list of databases.

Each of these online resources has its own strengths. The only way to learn what can and cannot be achieved is to test each one in several different ways. With the answers to the inventory questions presented earlier in this chapter, prepare a list of keywords for searching. These might include: preservation, outreach, collections, patient education, digitization, documentary, humanities, arts, STEM (science, technology, engineering, and mathematics), children's literature, and so forth. Experimenting by searching keywords is the first step. Some sponsors support programs from all over the country; others have specific geographic areas of focus, and others have preselected organizations that they support exclusively. Depending on the database searching options, another way to search is by entering the name of a similar library or parent organization to learn which sponsors have supported that organization, at what funding amounts, and for what types of projects or programs.

It is common when searching for funding sponsors and opportunities that initial results require additional research, so it is best to know some other options regarding how to learn more about what sponsors fund in order to deduce why certain projects match up with respective sponsors. Many foundations publish annual reports listing grantee organizations, funding amounts, and project titles; sometimes abstracts are included. Newspaper articles—local, regional, or national—routinely announce funding awards to grantees along with descriptions of awarded projects or programs. Film credits, concert guides, and public radio and television programs also share the names of sponsors that have contributed funds to support these productions.

Once a sponsor is selected, the learning begins. What is the sponsor's interest? Why did this sponsor choose to support its grantee awarded projects? How long has the sponsor been supporting this organization or this program? How much is the average award? Have award amounts changed in the past few years? Has the number of grantees increased or decreased recently? What's the geographical area of recent grantees and is there a pattern that favors regions or types of grantee organizations? These are appropriate questions to ask regarding any type of sponsor. The process of accumulating knowledge about a specific sponsor is akin to detective work, and librarians are perfect for the job!

To locate corporate sponsor giving opportunities for those corporations operating within a library's service area, simply create a list of appropriate corporations. Using search terms such as "_____ community giving program" and inserting the name of the corporation, the search will yield results that likely will lead the searcher to an online application form.

Produce a Master Deadline Schedule of Annotated Funding Opportunities and Deadlines

Searching for opportunities will inevitably result in actual funding opportunities that potentially match a library's focus or a librarian's interests. As the searches yield viable opportunities for librarians to pursue, relevant information should be captured while searching. As shown in table 4.1, it is best to create a Microsoft Excel spreadsheet that contains the following columns of information: deadline, funding agency, name of program, maximum amount of award, range of recent awards, description of award purpose(s), other details including length of grant period, and website link.

This document of information eventually will become the librarians' collective guide to possible sponsors. Sponsors usually update deadlines annually, with relatively few changes to program categories and funding purposes. Some sponsors, however, will completely change the patterns of giving from one year to the next, so it is important to visit sponsors' websites periodically. And, new program categories can pop up without much fanfare.

Some sponsors and online databases have added options to websites that allow for ongoing subscriptions to announcements about funding deadlines—also called requests for proposals (RFPs) or requests for applications (RFAs)—or for grant-related news stories. Subscribing to these posts can assist librarians in gathering information for inclusion in the master deadline schedule. For instance, by subscribing to the Institute of Museum and Library Services news blog, subscribers will be updated when awards are made with links to proposal abstracts organized by state, as well as announcements for deadlines, new programs, changes in guidelines and procedures, and general news important to libraries and museums. This is an excellent educational resource for those working to build a grants program.

Another good source of information is the Philanthropy News Digest (PND) (http://philanthropynewsdigest.org/rfps) published by the Foundation Center. Subscribers can select to receive RFP alerts related to forty-six specific disciplines of private funding opportunities such as elementary/secondary education, aging, community development, higher education, and health. A geographic option for identifying opportunities within a specific state is available. The website also features a tab called "RFPs," which provides the option of searching the PND complete list of opportunities and deadlines by discipline area (Foundation Center, 2015d).

Many academic institutions, through an office of research or sponsored programs, prepare and circulate an in-house newsletter listing impending funding opportunities. Librarians involved in updating a master deadline schedule should subscribe to this resource. The opportunities listed require the user to select a search category. These may include humanities, medicine, technology, science, or others. Any category or discipline,

Table 4.1. Entry of a Funding Opportunity within a Master Deadline Schedule

DEADLINE	FUNDING AGENCY	PROGRAM NAME	PURPOSES	FUNDING AMOUNT	OTHER DETAILS	LINK
3/28/2014	NN/LM	Express Outreach Project Awards	Encourage partnerships, community focused activities; improve access to electronic health information, promote and improve access to library and information services, use of technology for information access, etc.	Up to $6,000 for each project	No indirect costs are allowed. Funds must be spent by 4/30/14.	http:// nnlm .gov/sea/ funding/ expressout .html

of course, could be applicable to a library. Searching for appropriate grant opportunities for libraries and librarians can be a time-consuming process, so having access to quality information that already has been vetted for the general academic community is a good place to begin. Academic lists of available grants can enhance the work of librarians who also are searching for available grant notifications primarily targeted specifically to libraries, museums, or archives that likely will be excluded from academic funding opportunities. Consequently, a team approach to reviewing all the possible funding opportunities is best suited to cover the wide range of information.

Maintaining a master deadline schedule of funding opportunities is like caring for a plant. It requires regular attention to keep it alive and to retain its value long term. When updating is ignored, the result can cause librarians to become disinterested in the information gathering process. This can often be the initial cause for the decline of an organization's grants program.

Key Points

This chapter discusses the fundamental characteristics of the major types of sponsors, identifies resources for learning about funding opportunities and deadlines, and offers guidance on how to organize this information. With this information, libraries can begin to build a grant-seeking program that helps library personnel learn about appropriate external funding opportunities. You have learned that these fundamentals are important building blocks to identify sponsors and prepare to apply for external funding.

- Librarians are some of the best-skilled professionals when it comes to searching for funding opportunities and organizing search results for future use.
- There are several government granting agencies devoted to supporting libraries on a national, regional, and statewide basis.
- Public libraries need to be prepared to apply for private funding, which often requires an IRS letter of determination documenting proof of 501(c)(3) nonprofit charitable organization status.
- The type of money being awarded by the sponsor, whether private or public, dictates how grant funds can be spent.
- A master deadline schedule in a spreadsheet format can serve as a go-to resource of available funding information for a specific library's projects, programs, and facilities.

The next chapter outlines strategies for increasing the momentum of a library's grants program such that it offers library personnel options for learning about grantsmanship and applying what they have learned to more confidently apply for external funding.

References

Andrew W. Mellon Foundation. 2014. "Programs." Andrew W. Mellon Foundation. http://www .mellon.org/programs/.
Council on Foundations. 2015. "Foundation Basics." Council on Education. http://www.cof.org/ content/foundation-basics.

Foundation Center. 2015a. "Find Us—The Foundation Center's Funding Information Network." Foundation Center. http://foundationcenter.org/find-us.html.

———. 2015b. "Foundations Today Tutorial." Foundation Center. http://foundationcenter.org/getstarted/tutorials/ft_tutorial/what.html.

———. 2015c. "Guide to Funding Research: Funding Information Network." Foundation Center. http://foundationcenter.org/getstarted/tutorials/gfr/coop.html.

———. 2015d. "PND: Philanthropy News Digest." Foundation Center. http://philanthropynews digest.org.

———. 2015e. "Top Funders: 50 Largest Corporate Foundation by Total Giving." Foundation Center. http://foundationcenter.org/findfunders/topfunders/top50giving.html.

———. 2015f. "Top Funders: Top 100 U.S. Foundations by Asset Size." Foundation Center. http://foundationcenter.org/findfunders/topfunders/top100assets.html.

Hannon, Kerry. 2014. "Family Foundations Let Affluent Leave a Legacy." *New York Times*, February 10. http://www.nytimes.com/2014/02/11/your-money/family-foundations-let-affluent-leave-a-legacy.html.

IMLS (Institute of Museum and Library Services). 2015. "State Programs: Grants to State Library Administrative Agencies." Institute of Museum and Library Services. September 9. http://www.imls.gov/programs/.

IRS (Internal Revenue Service). 2014. "Compliance Guide for 501(c)(3) Private Foundations." Publication 4221-PF. Internal Revenue Service. http://www.irs.gov/pub/irs-pdf/p4221pf.pdf.

Walsh, Dennis. 2015. "Public Charity or Private Foundation—Why Does It Matter?" Planned Giving Design Center. June 15. http://www.pgdc.com/pgdc/public-charity-or-private-foun dation-why-does-it-matter.

Women's Funding Network. 2015. "About Us: A Growing Network, a Movement for Change." Women's Funding Network. September 15. http://www.womensfundingnetwork.org/about/.

CHAPTER 5

Ways to Grow a Culture of Grantsmanship

THIS CHAPTER PRESENTS A VARIETY of strategies that librarians can implement to inspire continued and growing involvement in a grants program. By leveraging the knowledge and information gathered from searching for external opportunities, librarians can now become active in preparing to apply to these sponsors. Individually, the strategies described in this chapter are simple to execute. When they are brought together under a grants program umbrella, library personnel can become progressively more prepared to take advantage of externally sponsored grant opportunities.

⊚ Create Workflow Checklists for Feasibility Review, Proposal Preparation, and Award Management

Far too often a library lacks written protocols for navigating the complicated process from identifying a possible grant opportunity to submission of a proposal. Some steps in the process are inherent and would apply to all grants. For example, regardless of what the specifics may be, every grants preparation system should include a mechanism to notify and appropriately include any personnel in the library system or administration who will be directly impacted by or involved in a grant award. Other steps are necessary for some sponsor applications but not for others. The more a written protocol encompasses all possible steps in navigating the process, the more helpful it will be to any library personnel involved.

Without a written protocol, librarians can expect to encounter discouraging difficulties during this process, especially when a deadline is looming. As an example, most librarians do not have the authority to simply prepare and submit a grant proposal for direct submission to a sponsor. This restriction actually benefits the librarian and protects the culture of grantsmanship within a library. The question then becomes: What is the process for developing and submitting a proposal that has the support of a library's administrators? An effective way to address this question while codifying the process is to develop workflow checklists describing all relevant activities to be accomplished by the appropriate participants or approvers for each activity.

Making complicated processes more transparent within a library reduces confusion. Libraries may have a variety of systems, departments, facilities, and employees that interact with any given grant proposal project. Because of these potential impacts, a proposed or funded grant project can easily create messy situations. Library personnel can become dissatisfied with grant projects in general. It can become unnecessarily stressful to become involved in preparing or managing a grant project.

As mentioned previously, grantsmanship is not a knowledge or skill typically found in libraries or in library science courses. It can be equated somewhat to the human resource procedures of hiring new personnel. Like grantsmanship, librarians may not have any experience or training in reviewing applicants or executing hiring procedures. As well, it may be a rare occurrence that a librarian serves on a hiring committee. As a result of these two factors, it's difficult to predict the outcome. If done well, it produces a long-term benefit for everyone. If not, the long-term exposure can be a serious liability.

In a discussion with Brian Keith, the Libraries' associate dean of faculty and administrative affairs at the University of Florida, he shared his perspectives on the benefits of using guided step-by-step procedures to manage a grant project development and management process. Creating this type of a written procedure for complex processes makes sense when multiple people are involved and when skill sets differ widely. Providing guided procedures positions the various personnel involved to focus and contribute their individual technical or subject-matter expertise. This type of documented procedure provides for administrative oversight that is not intrusive to these independent processes. They ensure that no one potentially impacted by or involved in the project creation or future execution is left out of the planning and review process prior to a proposal's submission. Most importantly, going forward, these step-by-step procedures provide the project leader with a firm assurance that organizational support is committed, and can be counted on if the project is actually awarded. In Keith's estimation, this is key to maintaining library-wide support for any grant-funded project. Maintaining good communication and information sharing about the activities and budget plans being developed along the way will avoid conflicts and surprises after the proposal has been submitted and potentially awarded.

A checklist for each phase of the grant project development, submission, and post-award management can serve to communicate the procedures that may be part of the process. These lists will reveal all the possible steps in a somewhat chronological order (though the chronology is likely to vary from one proposal to another). Preparing these checklists for library personnel will help everyone to visualize the steps to be accomplished immediately before and immediately after their particular involvement in the process—articulating all the invisible actions that occur behind the scenes in each phase. The design of checklists can take various forms depending on the number of people involved in managing the library. See appendix 5.1 for a sample of a workflow checklist.

Assessing project feasibility is the first phase of a grant development process. This phase includes actions from the point of idea inception and identification of a selected sponsor for supporting the project, through to the final step of determining whether or not the project idea, potential sponsor, and potential impact on the library are feasible and manageable. Some key steps to include in this checklist are:

- Develop a working title.
- Recruit a project team.
- Develop a summary of the project idea.
- Identify the sponsor and read the sponsor's guidelines.
- Prepare a customized checklist specifying all required documentation.
- Develop a draft timeline and budget for actualizing the project.
- Discuss the idea with the sponsor's program officer.
- Conduct a brainstorming session.
- Prepare a preliminary list of potential collaborating partners.
- Select, convene, and facilitate the feasibility review group (including project team members and respective supervisors, and other administrators) to determine project feasibility.

Each activity should identify persons responsible for participating in the respective activity.

Of the steps described, convening a feasibility review group to determine feasibility should be considered indispensable to preparing fundable proposals. Discussions should address questions such as:

- Why would the sponsor be interested in the proposed project?
- How will the project move the library forward to achieve its future plans?
- Will the budget sufficiently support the project?
- Does the project make sense for the library? Is it a good fit for the librarian leading the project and the project team members?
- Is the timing right to engage in the project, or would it be better if the project were delayed until next year?
- How would the project be strengthened if the team had more time?
- What other assets or library personnel could contribute to making this a stronger project?

These discussions are more important to developing a successful grants program than might be apparent at first glance. They serve many purposes. One purpose is to create opportunities to encourage buy-in, by those outside the project team, that otherwise can be difficult to generate. Participants in the feasibility review group who are not included in the project team may have access to resources that are inaccessible to the project team but can provide added value to a proposed project. Feasibility discussions offer a forum to advance the transparency of project ideas that might remain hidden until it is too late in the proposal development process to make changes. Furthermore, the discussions may result in a consensus that the project is infeasible or impractical. This decision can save the project team time and effort.

If the project is deemed to be feasible, the second phase of the grant development process is to prepare and submit the grant application. Important steps to include in this checklist are:

- Meet to further develop project plan ideas.
- Finalize the list of project team members.
- Assign application preparation responsibilities to project participants.
- Develop a list of cost share contributors and percent of time allocated to complete the project.
- Develop position descriptions for new positions related to the funding request.
- Update a short summary of the project description.
- Prepare and send an e-mail message to potential collaborators to secure letters of commitment.
- Prepare and send an e-mail message to potential consultants to secure letters of commitment.
- Prepare and send an e-mail message to potential writers of letters of support.
- Prepare and send an e-mail message to secure biographies and/or résumés for key personnel involved in the project.
- Identify potential vendors and secure bids.
- Determine if copyright clearance is necessary.
- Complete narrative sections.
- Finalize the project timeline, budget, and title.
- Prepare the budget narrative.
- Finalize attachments and the project abstract.
- Complete copyediting of all components.
- Confirm the project leader's receipt of all required résumés, letters, etc.
- Complete all required forms.
- Secure all required signatures and approvals.
- Submit the application package and receive confirmation of receipt.

The third and final phase of checklist-related activities is to manage the awarded project (also referred to as the post-award phase). Important activities to consider in the third phase would include:

- Upon written notification of an award from the sponsor, contact the grants coordinator or accountant.
- Complete and submit to the sponsor a revised budget if the award amount is not the full amount requested.

- Forward notification for processing the award and creating a separate account or project for managing and tracking grant funds.
- Read post-award grants management policies and procedures provided by the sponsor.
- Complete and submit fully executed agreements or documents required by the sponsor or to partnering applicant, if the library was not the actual applicant.
- Contact the project team and library administrators to announce the award.
- Confirm participation and commitment to serve on the project, as described in the proposal, with all collaborating organizations.
- If subcontractors, consultants, or vendors were included in the application, confirm commitment, role, and costs related to participation in the project.
- Prepare a news release, a list of media outlets, and publicize the awarded project.
- Convene a kickoff meeting with all project participants to officially start the project.
- As applicable, meet with appropriate staff or directors to discuss workflows, schedules, and other activities outlined in the proposal.
- If the budget includes voluntary or mandatory cost share contributions, then set up a tracking system to record and confirm this effort.
- If the budget includes travel, contact the appropriate staff member and proceed with travel coordination.
- Make calendar appointments for scheduled submissions for the sponsor's required interim and final reports, as applicable.
- Oversee completion of all activities listed in the timeline, as applicable.
- Receive and monitor monthly budget reports for the project, and oversee the budget and any payment schedules.
- Regularly convene project team members to keep everyone informed and to resolve any situations that may arise.
- Prepare and submit to the sponsor any required interim and final reports and other closeout documents.
- Prepare and submit a request for no-cost extension if more time is needed to complete the project, and if this is a provision offered by the sponsor.

When preparing the initial version of these procedural checklists, it is best to include every possible step in the feasibility review, application preparation, and post-award management process, regardless of whether the steps seem irrelevant at the time the checklists are first being prepared. Updating the checklists after every grant proposal feasibility determination, preparation and submission, and post-award grant management process helps to capture the new required activities appropriate for a library when these become known and applicable. As you can see, there are so many steps potentially involved in managing all of these phases that a librarian might struggle to remember all of the possibilities. Capturing and sharing all of the tasks that could possibly be required, from the conception of an idea to the completion of the project, will contribute to building confidence and competence in the successful acquisition and management of the library's grant awards.

Communicate Deadlines and Funding Opportunities

With the initial completion of entries to a master deadline schedule of external grant opportunities described in chapter 4, librarians have the necessary information to generate a funding alert e-mail message for their library or library system. The content of a funding alert should include the following:

- Title of the funding program, name of sponsoring agency
- Deadline date(s)
- Award amount(s): range or maximum
- A paragraph summarizing the type of projects or programs that are eligible for support
- Examples of types of projects or programs the sponsor typically funds, especially those related to library work
- Link to the guidelines and examples of awarded projects if available

As librarians increase the number of entries for funding opportunities in their master schedule, there will come a time when funding alerts can be circulated on a monthly basis. Readers will be most concerned with knowing upcoming deadlines. It is best to schedule the distribution of funding alert messages at least two to four months prior to a sponsor's deadline whenever possible. For example, a National Endowment for the Humanities (NEH) deadline for Digital Humanities Implementation Grants is September 16, 2015. The best time to share this funding opportunity in a funding alert message would be in June 2015. This will provide interested librarians with sufficient lead time to plan ahead of the deadline.

Because funding alerts will be scheduled for monthly distribution, in the case of the Digital Humanities NEH opportunity, the listing would be repeated in subsequent funding alerts in July, August, and September. As previously noted, a typical grant proposal requires at least forty hours of preparation after completing the feasibility process. So those planning to prepare funding alerts should be sensitive to the lead time needed to create interest in an opportunity, while at the same time providing sufficient preparation time to create a fundable application.

Each time a funding alert is circulated, the information included in the alert should be summarized and added to the master schedule. The schedule should be linked to a website or library guide to provide easy access and encouragement for users to discover and browse. It can be an excellent resource for grants committee members for referring mini-grant applicants whose projects may match up with a particular external sponsor's interests.

ⓖ Generate Customized Checklists for Funding Opportunities

Find and Interpret Sponsor Guidelines/Solicitations

When reviewing websites and databases for information on how to go about preparing a fundable application, in many cases the information will be clearly identifiable and understood. Most sponsors will provide a link to the guidelines, and within this material the information will be clear and direct. It also may be lengthy. Each sponsor has a different way of sharing its guidelines. An example is the National Science Foundation (NSF). By searching for "National Science Foundation guidelines," the link called "Grant Proposal Guide" will appear. This link takes the user to the *National Science Foundation Proposal and Award Policies and Procedures Guide* (http://www.nsf.gov/pubs/policydocs/pappguide/nsf15001/nsf15_1.pdf), which in part 1 provides the instructions for preparing proposals,

SAMPLE DESCRIPTION OF A GRANT
OPPORTUNITY TO BE INCLUDED IN A FUNDING ALERT

Library and Information Science Research Grant Program—OCLC/ALISE (OCLC Research, 2014)

Deadline: September 15
Award Amount: Up to $15,000 for one-year research project

In recognition of the importance of research to the advancement of librarianship and information science, OCLC and ALISE promote independent research that helps integrate new technologies that offer innovative approaches and contributes to a better understanding of the information environment and user expectations and behaviors.

Research related (but not limited) to the following areas is encouraged:

- The major OCLC research themes are listed here: http://www.oclc.org/research/activities.html
- Impact of digital technology on libraries, museums, and archives
- Social media, learning, and information seeking behavior
- New developments in knowledge organization (metadata, social tagging, linked data, etc.)

The following expense categories are eligible for direct funding:

- Release time from teaching for the principal investigator
- Research assistants
- Stipends
- Project-related travel
- Required attendance and presentation of research results at the 2017 ALISE Conference
- Equipment, if integral to the research
- Other research expenses

View a list of previous recipients and read their final papers and presentations: http://www.oclc.org/research/grants/awarded.htm.

Full guidelines are available here: http://oclc.org/research/grants/call.html (e.g., university staff, faculty, and students) and may be held in a password or IP-protected streaming media system.

and includes proposal review procedures and review criteria for all NSF programs (organized among seven research and education support directorates). Part 1 of the guide is eighty pages in length and should be read in its entirety to ensure the proposal will be prepared, packaged, and submitted correctly (NSF, 2014).

To find the guidelines for National Endowment for the Humanities funding programs, you can search for "NEH grant deadlines" and the resulting link (http://www .neh.gov/grants) will lead to a schedule listing all program titles and deadlines. Each program web page features a link to its respective guidelines. So in the case of NEH, grant applicants cannot assume that the guidelines for one program are appropriate to any other program.

The ALA Carnegie-Whitney Grant Program website (http://www.ala.org/offices/ publishing/sundry/alapubawrds/carnegiewhitney) will bring you to the guidelines web page. Unfortunately, this web page offers only part of the guidelines. At the bottom of the web page, the user will find three links: (1) "Proposal Requirements," (2) "Application Cover Sheet," and (3) "Responsibilities of Grant Recipients" (ALA, 2015). An applicant might assume that there is no need to review the third link because its title refers to post-award management procedures. But within the third link, an applicant will find a checklist with the order in which the sponsor wants to receive its application documents, which of course is information that would be helpful to have early in the preparation process.

These examples of sponsor guidelines illustrate the potential problems grant-seekers can create for themselves when making assumptions about the content they expect to find in the guidelines. Ensuring that all the guidelines have been located, read, and reread can make the difference between submitting a fundable proposal or one that will be declined.

Beyond locating guidelines, you must expect to find that guidelines can be

- inconsistent from one sponsor to another,
- contradictory about what exactly the sponsor requires, and
- written in such a way that may lead the reader to make incorrect assumptions.

Another common characteristic is that information about the criteria upon which applications will be evaluated inevitably will be located toward the back portions of the published guidelines. It often can be the case that a novice grant-writer may never discover the availability of review criteria if unaware of their existence. Some private sponsors don't include this information, and this can be very discouraging at times. This is not a deliberate act to make grant-seeking difficult. Rather, it is a fact of life in the grants world that not all guidelines are created equal.

Finding, reading and interpreting guidelines will be another activity librarians will want to practice and, eventually, master. The standard information typically found in proposal guidelines includes the following:

- Maximum award amounts
- Grant period, start and end dates for proposed funding
- Descriptions of eligible projects
- Allowable expenses
- Disallowable expenses
- Cover sheet and budget forms
- A list of narrative questions and content
- Checklist of all required materials for completing the application, in the order in which materials should be presented
- Instructions for when the application must be received, including the time of receipt on the deadline date, and where and how to submit the application

- Criteria for how applications will be reviewed
- Schedule of reviews and notification of awards

Create a Customized Grant Application Checklist for New Opportunities

As mentioned earlier, grant guidelines frequently include a checklist for applicants to ensure materials are included, organized, and submitted in the correct order. But this checklist should not be used as the default checklist for the applicant. It provides only the bare minimum of the content that is required for submission. A project team that has reached the point of seriously considering the pursuit of a specific opportunity, at this point, should be prepared to invest time in preparing the "container" for the proposal.

The mark of a well-prepared proposal is one which has followed guidelines in a way that addresses all the narrative components and all of the criteria for review. Given that each set of guidelines is unique, the activity of preparing the "container" for the proposal may require several hours. A container is healthy when it includes all the necessary components requested by the sponsor, as well as the review criteria, in the form of questions to be answered, rather than statements. The structure and language of guidelines often is presented in the form of statements, such as: "Describe the significance of the project in relation to its impact on the humanities." Or: "Provide a description of the audiences the project will serve." Criteria also are presented in the form of statements, such as: "The degree to which the project will meet the needs of its target audience."

Directional statements like these fail to provide a project team with what is needed to generate a well-prepared fundable proposal. To achieve this result, the team or the librarian leading the effort should convert the statements required for the narrative and those articulated in the criteria into well-formulated questions. This will present several challenges, the most important of which is deciding where to insert the answers to questions related to each criterion. The following instructions provide general guidance on how to prepare a customized checklist for preparing a proposal that conforms to the sponsor's guidelines and review criteria, while customizing the checklist to match up with a proposed project.

1. Print and read the entire guidelines document, and search for other information the sponsor shares online, to ensure access to every possible form of instruction, policy, or guidance.
2. Highlight all instructions for preparing and submitting the proposal.
3. Create a checklist template (see appendix 5.2, "Sample Grant Application Checklist"). Search for the order in which the sponsor wants each document to be presented within the application package.
4. Using the sponsor's prescribed order, begin entering each component into the checklist. Delay inserting the person responsible for completing each section until all of the required documentation and notes have been entered.
5. While reviewing the instructions for narrative content, begin converting each instructional statement into a question. If the sponsor's guidelines include narrative questions, then simply insert these questions into the checklist. The goal is to fully inform the reviewer with information that builds confidence in the applicant as being worthy of an award. It may be necessary to craft additional questions that will generate responses to better achieve this goal. It also may be necessary to add questions specifically designed to inquire about a library's unique assets as they

relate to the proposed project, including collections, audiences, programs, services, or facilities. This ensures that the narrative features a library's distinctive assets that reviewers can learn more about as they read through the proposal. Questions should drive the content of the narrative, creating a container in which to place the responses. The desired effect will be that as reviewers read the narrative responses, sans the underlying questions, they will continue to accumulate information throughout the review with interest and excitement about what they are learning. The quality of the application narrative is directly related to the quality of the questions within the checklist.

6. Locate the criteria reviewers will be using to evaluate the proposal. Just as in step 5, convert each criterion into a question or questions, as needed. Review the narrative questions already placed within the checklist and determine where to embed each criterion question for the best fit. Distribute all the criteria questions within the narrative sections, appropriately, to ensure that responses will obviously speak to each criterion as the reviewer reads through it. This in combination with step 5 is the most important step of the grant preparation process—yes, the MOST IMPORTANT step—and should take whatever time is necessary to strategically and thoroughly complete.

7. Continue entering the other required content, which will follow the narrative in the order outlined by the sponsor's guidelines. These may include such content as schedule of completion, budget, budget justification, letters of commitment to participate in the project, letters of support that validate the quality of the project, and appendixes with content that presents additional information related to narrative content.

8. Once all of the required content and questions related to criteria have been embedded in the checklist, the next step is to add any notes that clarify the requirements. These include page limitations, word or character limitations, font and margin requirements, whether a sponsor's form is required, the required names of each file document to be uploaded, and so forth.

9. It will be important, at this point, to meet with the project team to flesh out the "persons responsible" portions of the checklist.

Each time another grant opportunity has been discovered that matches a specific project a librarian would like to pursue, a new customized application checklist should be generated. Regardless of whether the application gets submitted, if a checklist was created for a specific funding opportunity, most of its content will be relevant for reuse in a subsequent application cycle. Only the new or updated requirements will need to be added. Over time, as more and more checklists are generated, librarians will find themselves increasingly well prepared to respond to application deadlines due to the availability of customized checklists. A sample of a customized application checklist is available in appendix 5.2.

Hands-On Activities to Demystify Grant-Writing Processes

Locate and Mine Funded Proposals

Having access to actual awarded proposals is one of the best ways to learn how to present information about a proposed project within the container of a grant application. Some awarded applications can be found online. Government sponsors sometimes share digital examples of successful applications within their respective websites. This is the case for programs within the National Endowment for the Humanities and the Institute for Museum and Library Services. It also is a best practice for grantees to provide links to awarded proposals on websites created to disseminate information about their awarded projects, or on web pages related to the online project product resulting from sponsor funding. Furthermore, some applications can sometimes be found online in institutional repositories created and maintained by academic libraries. These online sources may or may not contain the full application package. For instance, the budget is more likely to be included if the applicant is a governmental entity and its personnel salaries and benefit information are already publicly available. Usually application budget amounts have been redacted or the budget is excluded. Appendixes also are often excluded from online access.

Other options exist for viewing funded proposals if not included in a sponsor's website or an institutional repository. In the case of government grants, a program officer assisting a librarian with developing a fundable project idea or strategy may offer, or agree if asked, to share digital copies of funded proposals similar to the project being proposed. Or the sponsor may provide the librarian with a contact person from whom a copy of an awarded proposal can be requested. Most public sponsors prefer that awarded applications be obtained directly from the applicant. If an applicant cannot be located or refuses to share the proposal, public sponsors will share these pursuant to the Freedom of Information Act.

For privately funded proposals, the only means of accessing copies is to contact the applicant directly. A program officer may suggest that you contact an applicant whose proposal was funded some years earlier and does not conflict with a currently funded project. Or it may be that a program officer is aware of the willingness of an applicant organization to share proposals freely and will provide a contact for requesting an electronic copy.

Both public and private sponsors, as well as applicants, share information about awarded projects, whether through online news postings, blogs, websites, newspapers, or through IRS 990 forms. There is much to be gained if a librarian discovers an awarded project of interest and is willing to spend time searching for the grantee contact. This extra effort may yield benefits beyond simply obtaining a copy of a previously funded proposal. A grantee project leader may be willing to share lessons learned about executing the project, offer resources of assistance, or even volunteer to cooperate or collaborate on the project being developed. This is especially true if the grantee organization is another library.

Design and Facilitate Grant-Training Workshops

Another essential activity for promoting a culture of grantsmanship is to design and facilitate grant-training workshops. The most effective workshops are those that provide practical experiences for participants, rather than focusing on theoretical concepts. You don't need to be an expert in grant-seeking to facilitate grants-related training workshops. Some examples of workshop strategies and methods are provided here to help you visualize the content and activities.

Mock Review Panel Workshop

The goal of this workshop is to simulate the review process, conducted by sponsors and grant review panels, to determine which applicants will be awarded and which will be declined. Prepare for the workshop by gathering three to five grant applications submitted by librarians or library applicant organizations. Budgets need not be included, but applications should contain as much of the narrative as is available. Workshop participants will benefit if all the applications were submitted to the same sponsor, but it doesn't matter if they were not funded through the same program. Make printed copies of all the applications, preferably opting for two-sided copies to condense applications.

Divide workshop participants, which may include only librarians or a mix of library personnel, into small groups of three to five participants. Distribute applications so that each participant receives a copy of every application. Distribute highlighting markers to each participant. Instruct groups to brainstorm a list of possible criteria that can easily be used to evaluate each application. These might include: the degree to which the application is convincing; or whether the project being proposed is innovative, evidence-based, or feasible. Through a facilitated debriefing of criteria options, the large group then determines four or five general criteria that can be applied to most applications, even those proposing planning or research projects. They also decide on a numerical scoring system for evaluating proposals based on the selected four or five criteria.

Next, direct participants to read and evaluate applications using the highlighters to designate sentences and phrases that support a criterion or that hook the reader into becoming interested in the proposed project. Applications should take no longer than fifteen minutes to review. When all applications have been read and highlighted, one by one, applications are discussed for their respective strengths and weaknesses in relation to the criteria. Finally, participants determine scores for each of the reviewed applications. Groups then determine the average score for each proposal, sharing these group scores with the other groups in a large-group debriefing presentation. The facilitator keeps track of each group score and then averages the scores based on the number of groups to determine the ranking of applications, from highest to lowest scores.

Funding Analysis Workshop

The goal of this workshop is to practice determining the rationale behind why proposals were awarded by sponsors. Prepare for the workshop by finding and printing out an announcement of awarded grant titles and abstracts published by NEH, IMLS, state libraries, or other sponsors for awards submitted by libraries or archives. After distributing the list of awarded projects, participants are instructed to team up into pairs. Pairs then read the announced awards looking for patterns or other discoveries about the awards. One discovery might be that the state of California received the most awards, or that digital projects were among the most successful in receiving awards. Analyzing award amounts and any patterns that can be discerned also is a worthwhile activity. After all the participant pairs have completed their analyses, the facilitator leads a discussion of the findings where pairs present their discoveries to the larger group. This workshop can be modified to analyze funding patterns within a specific funding program, say, all of the state LSTA awards and awardees.

Preparing a Specific Component of a Grant Application Workshop

"How-to" trainings for preparing the various components of documentation required in grant applications can provide substantial assistance, especially to new grant-seekers. A workshop that addresses the theme of how to create a statement of significance, for example, can greatly improve the way librarians prepare this portion of an application.

Prepare for the workshop by gathering a variety of examples from funded or declined grant or fellowship (funding for individuals) applications. Narratives justifying the importance or relevance of the project are often required by the sponsor. Only the section marked "Significance," "Project Importance," or "Need Being Addressed" should be copied for distribution, along with highlighters, to workshop participants. Sharing, if it is possible, a declined version and also a version that has been revised and awarded for the same project, will be instructive when comparing the two versions.

Direct participants to highlight those phrases or sentences that strongly articulate the project's value to the field or to a specific community of beneficiaries. They can then exchange their highlighted documents with each other, sharing their analysis for a larger group discussion about why certain applications were stronger than others. Participants also can be directed to generate the types of questions for which answers were found in the applications—namely, the answers that contributed to developing a convincing statement of significance. The same type of workshop can be redesigned to be instructive in the creation of other application elements including timelines, budgets, biographies, evaluation methods, and so forth.

Showcase of Grant-Funded Projects

This workshop provides an exceptional method for sharing the results of grant-funded projects within a library. Projects can include mini-grants, library partnership projects where the library is not the applicant organization, and fellowship or travel awards received by individual librarians, as well as awarded grants made to a library or librarian by external sponsors for planning or project implementation. A showcase workshop should present information about the results of either a single project or of many projects.

The key to this type of workshop is to have all presenters share answers to the following recommended questions: What was the project and why was it important to undertake? What went well during the project? What difficulties were encountered and how were these resolved? What did the project team learn from participating in the project? What would the project leader or team have done differently to make the project more successful or efficient? What were the results of the project, and what will be its future impact?

Presentations can take from about three to ten minutes with additional time allocated for audience Q&A. Showcasing completed grant-funded projects can generate interest, enthusiasm, and greater participation in a library's grants program.

Serve on Grant Review Panels

External sponsors regularly request nominations for those interested in serving on grant review panels. These opportunities afford librarians a very beneficial learning experience in terms of acquiring grantsmanship knowledge. Any form of panel or committee whose charge is to review applications, deliberate, and select awardees will suffice. Examples include panels such as those reviewing scholarship applications, travel grants to faculty, or academic technology awards. A university campus may have several internal review committees that allocate funding awards based on applications. Community foundations or United Way agencies also are excellent external sponsors that use formal review processes that include community representation. State agencies also look for peer reviewers through a nomination process. On a national level, federal agencies are perpetually seeking grant reviewers, including IMLS, NEH, NIH, NSF, Corporation for National and Community Service, and many others.

Selecting a panel on which to submit a nomination application should be based on a librarian's past experience. Usually three to five years of experience or service in the field for which a panel is being convened is a prerequisite. For instance, if a librarian has established and managed a lecture series of author presenters, this experience may qualify for service on literature panels convened by a state's arts council. Or, a librarian with extensive digital humanities experience may have the desired experience to serve on digital project planning or implementation grant review panels at the NEH. Public librarians are often involved in creating and presenting public programs, and these experiences also may be sufficient to serve on NEH panels for public programs.

Reviewing proposals can be daunting, but there are ways to make the process more efficient and enjoyable. Here are some tips to begin the task of reviewing a stack of applications:

1. Read the guidelines designed for applicants to get a clear idea of the requirements and how criteria for review have been articulated.
2. Ensure a review sheet has been printed for each application and note the title of each project.
3. Review one proposal to estimate how much time each proposal will take to review, then set up a schedule to ensure all applications can be reviewed prior to the panel's deadline.

When reviewing proposals, begin by reading the budget and the budget narrative. This will provide you with valuable information about how funds will be expended if the application is awarded. With this information in mind, turn to the timeline to review the activities planned for the project, if a timeline or Gantt chart is provided. Next, read the abstract of the project, the narrative sections, and all the attachments.

If an audit report is included for organization applicants, review this first, prior to the budget. A certified audit will provide an abundance of information related to an organization's financial condition. The auditor's opinion letter may indicate that the report includes a "qualified opinion" due to lack of evidence or variances in standard accounting practices. In this case, it could be that the applicant organization's internal controls or accounting procedures are inadequate; this should be a concern for reviewers. Learning to read and comprehend audit documents and budgets is important for any review panelist.

Knowing the budget and timeline information prior to reviewing the narrative sections of the application can help reduce the number of times a reviewer has to reread the narrative. It also helps to discern whether the proposed project matches well with the rationale for its budget and timeline. It is sometimes the case that these elements don't align, and it's important to catch this during review. While reviewing each application write notes on the actual application and on a separate note sheet, not on the official review sheet. This will help you to see quickly where the application is strong or weak.

Once all the applications have been reviewed, organize the proposals in preference order, from best to worst. Assign scores according to the review criteria, and then add comments to the review sheet that include both positive attributes of the application as well as those that provide recommendations for improvement or that point out deficiencies. Some reviewers decide not to share anything more than a score. This limits greatly what applicants can learn from the grant preparation process, and if the proposal is declined, there is often little to be gained from the experience. On the other hand, thorough review comments can be illuminating for the project teams who have prepared them.

During the panel review meeting, be prepared to share review scores and comments that justify the rationale for each score. Reviewers will be very interested in learning how others have scored the applications. In some review sessions, a reviewer will be selected to represent specific applications by giving a synopsis of the project and then leading the discussion of strengths and weaknesses. Listening attentively and keeping track of the scores of other reviewers will help to either validate a reviewer's scores or generate a discussion of the disparity in the scores. Some processes include the elimination of the highest and lowest scores prior to averaging scores as a means for eliminating aberrant discrepancies. Regardless of the particular review process, being well prepared for the review session will make for a very rewarding and educational experience.

Participate as a Partner on a Grant Project

Librarians and libraries don't always have to serve as the official grant applicant; rather, supporting a partnering organization's application can produce mutual benefits. A librarian should give serious consideration, if given the opportunity, to participate in a collaborative project with a viable lead applicant, whether it is a library, nonprofit organization, or academic entity. Essentially, by participating in collaborative projects, a librarian or group of library employees can add significant value to any proposal. Example roles may include acting as convener for community discussions or presentations, contributing to a collaborative digital collection, providing training to community participants, or disseminating information about health or other community resources. For novice grant-seekers, partnering with a previously successful applicant can help to introduce the grant-seeking process without necessitating all the extra work required by an applicant.

Ensuring that adequate funding is being allocated to cover the library's costs of participation in a collaborative project should be a consideration in every collaborative grant opportunity. In some cases, the product of the project itself is so important to a library or its constituents that funding for a librarian's or library staff's efforts is less critical. Offering time as an in-kind contribution should also be considered, whether or not funds are allocated in the budget for partnership participation. Contributed effort by librarians or library staff will make a collaborative proposal more competitive in that libraries are generally considered to be trustworthy partners.

⊚ Report Grant Activities

Informing a library's stakeholders of its grant activities achieves many purposes. It primarily contributes to the transparency of all grant-seeking activities while acknowledging the work of project leaders and teams who have contributed to an application's development, regardless of the ultimate funding results. Such reports increase the enthusiasm for submitting grant proposals simply by sharing all the particulars about these applications. It is typically the case that the entire library staff are only informed about awarded grant projects, usually through a message from the library director's office congratulating a project leader and team. But this method excludes the conveyance of information about all the other grant applications that were submitted and subsequently declined. The assets resulting from these "failed" attempts thereby become discarded rather than shared and leveraged for future opportunities simply by withholding information about all submitted proposals.

It is important for libraries to ensure that information about all grant applications—including those submitted by partnering organizations where librarians are contributing effort—are acknowledged at the time of submission. Librarians or the grants management committee members should develop a method for capturing and sharing this information. A grants activities report, circulated library-wide on a monthly or quarterly basis, can serve this purpose well. It should provide information for each submitted, pending, awarded, or declined application (except for internally funded mini-grant applications, which should only include those which were awarded). Because this report includes information about declined proposals submitted to external sponsors, circulating the report beyond a library's staff and board members could have detrimental effects on those who were involved in its preparation and submission. An alternative means of communicating information to those beyond a library is to maintain a website that shares summaries of all awarded projects.

An internal library grants activities report can include the following information:

- The title of the project
- A summary of the project's objectives
- Amount of cash request and in-kind contribution
- The start and end dates proposed for the grant period
- The project leader and members of the project team
- Name of the sponsor and program category
- A link to the full proposal

A sample of an entry in a grants activity report is shown in the textbox.

RECENTLY AWARDED

"Women Authored Science Books for Children 1790–1890: An Annotated Bibliography" (122435)—($5,000 cash request; $6,736 cost share)

This project seeks to research and design a digital annotated bibliography of 200 primarily non-fiction science books written by women for children between 1790 and 1890. This will be the first project to create an annotated bibliography of an important topic within the collection. The project plan is to: 1) select 200 titles from the Baldwin Library based on date, authorship, reputation of author, scarcity, cultural impact (if known), and condition; 2) conduct research focusing on specific titles, themes, authors, and cultural significance through a contract with literature expert, Alan Rauch, Ph.D., professor of English at the University of North Carolina—Charlotte; 3) design the format of the annotated bibliography to meet online user requirement needs; 4) using research results, write annotations with notes for multiple editions where appropriate; 5) promote the completed bibliography; and, 6) evaluate usage and benefits once the project is complete. (Project team: S. Alteri [PI], and D. Van Kleeck) (start date: 3/1/15; end date: 2/28/17) ALA Carnegie-Whitney Grant Program [includes a hyperlink to the actual proposal].

This type of report offers another way to fuel interest in a library's grant-seeking program. Fiscal administrators benefit by having all of the relevant information in one place as a quick reference tool. Project leaders and teams benefit by being reminded of the project's goals and objectives, while the sponsor deliberates the fate of the application, which prevents overextending commitments to other tasks in the meantime. Library administrators benefit from having access to all pending and active grant descriptions for future planning purposes. Because the report is circulated to all library stakeholders, it demonstrates the commitment of the library to grant-seeking activities and to those who participate in these processes. In time, stakeholders will look forward to routinely receiving grant activity reports and learning of the progress being achieved.

Key Points

This chapter discusses a variety of ways to nurture a grants program. You have learned some important ways to provide encouragement to those interested in developing such a supportive program.

- Checklists provided by sponsors may not fully outline all of the required content and documentation of a complete fundable proposal.
- Criteria for how your proposal will be reviewed should be an important component of each proposal preparation checklist.
- Procedures for all the steps required to prepare and submit grant applications within your library system will increase understanding and transparency about the grants preparation process.
- Short descriptions and results of external grant submissions, including declinations, can inspire support for a library's grants program.
- Grant-training workshops that analyze awarded grant documents are options for providing hands-on practical learning experiences.
- When a librarian serves as a partner on a grant application, his or her involvement can enhance the application's competitiveness.

The next chapter outlines major components that are typically found in grant applications and the purpose that each component serves in the review process, along with recommendations on how to prepare them.

Appendix 5.1: Sample Workflow Checklist to Assess Feasibility

PROJECT TITLE: _____

PART I: GRANTS PREPARATION CHECKLIST—ASSESS FEASIBILITY TASKS—PAGE 1 OF 2	PI AND CO-PIS	GRANTS MANAGER	HR / FISCAL SERVICES	PROJECT PARTICIPANTS	DIRECT SUPERVISORS OF PI / CO-PI	CHAIRS OF PI / CO-PI	ASSOC. DEANS OF PROJECT PARTICIPANTS	DEAN
1. Create working title sufficient to communicate the project to internal and external stakeholders.	X	X						
2. Create working summary of project (2 to 3 paragraphs) for communicating the idea to program officer or internal/external stakeholders.	X	X						
3. If sponsor and program have not been identified, research funding opportunities calendars and past funding alerts, FYI newsletter, IRIS and other databases found in Funding LibGuide.	X	X						
4. Read program guidelines and prepare list of questions for soliciting clarification.	X	X						
5. As necessary, obtain clarification of sponsor's guidelines and procedures.	X	X						
6. Research past awards made by the identified sponsor: award amount, project theme priorities, region of the country, scale of projects, etc.	X	X						
7. Determine application deadline, and cost share (matching funds) requirement.	X	X						
8. Determine whether IDC [indirect cost] is allowable, if not, whether it should be used for cost share.	X							
9. Prepare customized sponsor checklist of requirements in question form, including the sponsor's evaluation criteria, within appropriate narrative sections (sample checklist).	X	X						
10. Prepare preliminary timeline of major activities required to execute project.	X	X						
11. Establish list of required resources: personnel, OPS, vendors, student labor, supplies, equipment, travel, etc. Note: If project involves digitization, conservation, storage, exhibits, cataloging, copyright issues, or other activities outside of PI's unit, then appropriate staff and/or chairs must be consulted and included in Feasibility Group[1] and eventual Project Team.[2]	X	X						
12. As applicable, meet with appropriate staff or chairs to discuss projects for activities outside the PI's unit to determine costs and/or issues: project: · digitization · conservation · storage · exhibits · cataloging · copyright	X	X		X				

#	Task	PI AND CO-PIS	GRANTS MANAGER	HR / FISCAL SERVICES	PROJECT PARTICI- PANTS	DIRECT SUPER- VISORS OF PI / CO-PI	CHAIRS OF PI / CO-PI	ASSOC. DEANS OF PROJECT PARTICIPANTS	DEAN
13.	Identify Feasibility Group and schedule meeting.	X	X						
14.	Prepare preliminary budget estimate to determine feasibility of project vis-à-vis selected sponsor's grant history and guidelines, and importance to Libraries' mission. Determine costs related to each unit's involvement in the project.	X	X	X					
15.	Determine if there is a need/case for waiving or reducing IDC (in rare instances).	X	X	X					X
16.	Determine if program officer should be contacted to secure feedback and advice about project purpose, budget, etc., and contact as necessary.	X	X						
17.	Determine list of collaborating entities beyond the Libraries necessary and possibly interested in participating as supporters, leaders, or in other roles to give project credibility, expand audiences, perform tasks based on expertise not available in the Libraries, create multiple layers of benefits and beneficiaries, etc.	X	X		X				
18.	Determine scholars who may be necessary and interested in participating as supporters, advisors, consultants, or in other roles.	X			X				
19.	Contact potential collaborators and/or scholars to determine interest in potential project.	X							
20.	Based upon information gathered above, convene Feasibility Group meeting to secure feedback and assess feasibility, and/or create list of pending questions. If competing proposals are planned for the same sponsor, this may require discussions with Associate Deans and Dean.	X	X		X	X	X	X	
21.	If deemed to be a feasible project, use feedback to:								
	• Confirm Project Team, PI, and Co-PI	X			X	X	X	X	
	• Update summary (4 to 5 paragraphs)	X	X		X				
	• Update preliminary budget	X	X	X					
22.	Review updated summary and preliminary budget.	X	X	X	X	X	X	X	

◎ Appendix 5.2: Sample Grant Application Checklist

Derived from the 2014 program guidelines for National Endowment for the Humanities, Digital Humanities Start-Up Grants

Deadline: September 2014; notification in March 2015
Projects beginning in May for up to 18 months, awards from $30K to $60K

Preparer(s)	Requirement
☐	Application for Federal Domestic Assistance (grants.gov)
☐	Supplementary Cover Sheet (grants.gov)
☐	Project/Performance Site Locations Form (grants.gov)
☐	Table of contents
☐	List of participants
☐	Abstract (one page): Activities and expected results
☐	Plus 2 Statements: Innovation Significance; Humanities Significance (500 characters each)

[**Narrative sections**: (no jargon) single spaced, 1" margins, minimum 11 point font, Level I: 3 pages; Level II: 6 pages]

☐	**I. Enhancing the Humanities Through Innovation**

- What are the start activities?
- What are the ultimate project results?
- What is the value to scholars, students and general audiences in the humanities?
- What's the scope of project activities?
- What are the major issues or research questions to be addressed?
- What is the significance to the humanities?
- Why is the proposed methodology compatible with the intellectual goals of the project and the expectation of future users of the product?
- What's the project's potential for enhancing research, teaching and learning?
- What's the evidence of innovation in terms of the quality of the project idea, approach, method, or digital technology, and the appropriateness of the technology employed?

Preparer(s)	Requirement
☐	**II. Environmental Scan**

- What similar work in the humanities is being done in this area of study? How does this work relate to the proposed project?

- What similar software has been developed for other projects?
- How does the proposed project solution differ?
- How will current software be adapted and re-used for the proposed project?
- What are the pros and cons of adapting and reusing existing software?
- How does the proposed project contribute to and advance the field?
- What is the evidence that suggests likelihood the project will stimulate or facilitate new research of value to scholars and general audiences in the humanities? ... or ... What is the evidence suggesting a likelihood that scholars and general audiences will use new digital technologies to communicate humanities scholarship to broad audiences?

III. History and Duration of the Project

- What is the project's history, preliminary research or planning, previous related work, previous financial support, publications produced, and previously available resources or research facilities?
- What are the plans to continue beyond the end of the grant period?
- What are probable sources of support for subsequent phases?
- What is the evidence of the quality of the concept, organization, and definition of the project?

IV. Work Plan

- What are the specific tasks to be accomplished during the grant period?
- What computer technology will be employed?
- Which staff members will be involved?
- What technical resources will be required?
- How will results be evaluated? What was accomplished during the grant period? How will the long-term project goals be achieved?
- (If staging a workshop or conference, include application, agenda, list of proposed participants)
- What is the evidence of the work plan feasibility and whether it can achieve its stated goals during the grant period?

V. Staff

- List everyone: roles/responsibilities, percent of effort for project director and collaborators
- If an advisory group is part of the project, what is its function, and who are the members?
- What is the evidence of the quality of commitment of the project leader, staff and contributors?
- One paragraph biographies for each principal project participant
- Provide a statement of function and list of advisory group members if applicable.
- What is the evidence of quality of expertise and qualifications of the project leader, staff and contributors?

Preparer(s)	Requirement

☐   **VI. Final Product and Dissemination**

- What are the plans to disseminate the project results?
- What media will be used?
- How will your project's white paper detail the activities of the project?
- What potential usefulness to the field will come as a result of the white paper?
- NOTE: New software should be made freely available in every sense of the term, including the use, copying, distribution, and modification of the software. Open-source software or source code should preferably be made available through SourceForge or GitHub.

☐   Project budget

☐   Budget narrative (optional if needed)

☐   Federally negotiated IDC cost rate agreement

☐   **Data Management Plan**

- How will the team manage and disseminate data generated or collected by the project?

☐   Letters of commitment (one from each partner authorizing official)

☐   Letters of support from outside UF experts in this type of project importance and benefits (no more than 2)

Appendices (no more than 10 pages total)

☐   Workshop or meeting agendas, as applicable

☐   Bibliography

☐   Wireframes, as applicable

☐   Screen shots, as applicable

☐   Other project schematics, as applicable

☐   Schedule of completion

☐   Job descriptions for each new employee

⑥ References

ALA (American Library Association). 2015. "The Carnegie-Whitney Grant Guidelines." http://www.ala.org/offices/publishing/sundry/alapubawrds/carnegiewhitney.

NSF (National Science Foundation). 2014. "Proposal and Award Policies and Procedures Guide." December 26. http://www.nsf.gov/pubs/policydocs/pappguide/nsf15001/nsf15_1.pdf.

OCLC Research. 2014. "OCLC/ALISE Library & Information Science Research Grants." February 24. http://www.oclc.org/research/grants.html.

CHAPTER 6

Strategies for Completing Application Components

THIS CHAPTER PRESENTS STEP-BY-STEP recommendations for tackling the individual components typically found in proposals. As mentioned previously, application guidelines will be different from one program to another and from different sponsors. The content provided in chapter 5 delivers a basic road map to follow in terms of organizing the work and workflows, regardless of the application being prepared. In contrast, chapter 6 dissects each component typically required by sponsors, to complete a grant application package.

Hypothetically, assume a librarian has identified a sponsor whose funding priorities and deadline match up perfectly with a particular project idea and time frame. The librarian has prepared the customized checklist itemizing all the required documentation and accompanying questions to be answered, including those responding to the sponsor's criteria as described in chapter 5. Project team members have been confirmed, and a feasibility group has determined that the project is viable and should move ahead. The next step would be to establish how the items on the checklist should be prepared.

Less experienced grant-writers commonly make the error of completing forms and writing narrative sections in the order in which these appear in the sponsor's guidelines. To provide a more efficient approach that yields better results, the arrangement of topics in this chapter is based on the recommended order in which proposals should be prepared. The chapter content should be used in combination with the section in chapter 5 titled "Create a Customized Grant Application Checklist for New Opportunities."

Regardless of the grant application content, librarians preparing grant applications must keep the reviewers' needs at the forefront of their minds. What matters most is that the application engages and interests the reviewer, and that all the components come together in a cohesive way to give each reviewer confidence in the applicant, its project team, and its partners. In the end, the quality of the proposal most often will be judged by complete strangers and they are the customers whom the proposal must convince.

◎ Prepare a Grant Application Work Plan

The application work plan is the foundation of any grant proposal. It is the glue that holds the entire presentation of information together. Occasionally a work plan is not a required component of the application package. Regardless, a work plan is a prerequisite for any well-written proposal, and a tool for creating a budget that accurately reflects the project's activities and necessary costs, whether it gets included in the application package or not.

The purpose of a work plan is to demonstrate to the reviewer that the project team has spent sufficient time and contributed expertise to coherently propose how and when the project will be actualized. Of course this is all conjecture. But just like any plan, it should convincingly convey that the applicant knows how best to execute the project. This does not mean including every small action step, but rather the major activities the project team proposes to complete. It also should include the time frame in which the activities will occur and the person(s) responsible to lead and carry out each activity.

In terms of the time frame, it is best to describe activities that will be occurring only during the sponsor's announced grant period. Within the guidelines, a sponsor will indicate when awarded projects can begin and a date by which the project must be completed. This is known as the grant period. The work plan should not include action steps that are planned to occur prior to or after the grant period. This practice allows reviewers to focus only on activities proposed to be included in the project budget. By including activities outside the grant period, an applicant can confuse the reviewer, who may question the actual activities to be supported by the sponsor's awarded funds.

Descriptions of activities that will occur, or have already occurred in the margins of the grant period, should be shared in the narrative, if space permits. Relevant project activities that have been completed or are in process at the time an application is being prepared can be described in a section titled "Background" or "History of the Project." Reviewers will want to know not only what an applicant has completed in terms of project preparation, planning, assessment, or completion of a pilot project, but also what the applicant plans to complete prior to the beginning of the grant period—while applications are being processed and reviewed. It is typical that government grant applications can take between six and nine months to be reviewed and officially awarded or declined. This is a long time for a project to potentially remain stagnant. Information about this no-man's-land period can be included as a note introducing the work plan, or within the project history section, if this section exists. Activities planned to be performed after the grant period can be placed following the work plan description. Using a heading that clarifies that these activities will be performed after the grant period has ended provides a means for describing how the project will be sustained.

Work plans and timelines can be documented in a variety of formats. Sometimes an application can be enhanced by including a work plan—for example in narrative format—accompanied by a chart that illustrates a visual time frame. In this case, if the number of narrative pages prohibits inclusion of both versions within the narrative, another option would be to include the chart as an appendix item, if the guidelines allow.

Regardless of the chosen format, the applicant should strive to communicate the project's activities in such a way that the timeline accurately conveys a mental movie of the project in the minds of reviewers. If reviewers are able to visualize the project unfolding and progressing throughout the grant period, then the applicant has accomplished a notable achievement. When reviewers grapple to create a mental movie of the project plan with little success, this gap in clarity makes reviewing the entire proposal difficult. The inability to visualize project activities in a cohesive fashion likely will be reflected in the reviewers' scores.

Another important characteristic of the work plan is that the content included must be realistic and feasible. Reviewers will question as they read: Is this time frame achievable? Are the right people involved? Are these steps in the most efficient chronological order? Are some steps unnecessary? Is the time frame sufficient?

Some librarians will find it challenging to imagine all of the major project development and management activities that need to be completed to successfully execute the project. This can be overcome with practice and through the contributions of colleagues on a project team, or by engaging participants during a brainstorming session. Working collaboratively to discover all the major steps—and their respective sequence, dependencies, length of time to complete, and identified individuals required to perform these tasks—is a common requirement of any project development planning process.

A narrative style is a commonly used method for describing a project work plan within a grant application. This style can easily accommodate activities in large chunks of time (e.g., quarterly or biannually). The use of headings for the time frame combined with bullets to differentiate the activities can be very effective. This method works well when it accommodates inclusion of persons responsible for the various activities, which makes the plan easier to visualize.

Quarter 1 (July–Sep. 2012):

- Advisory Board (Advisors) meets first time in St. Augustine with PI, UF curators, and partners, and establishes selection guidelines to be used throughout the project.

Advisors begin selecting 1,500 items from St. Augustine Historical Society and P.K. Yonge Library of Florida History collections. Advisors and curators will consult with UF conservator (Freund) to assess archival materials to be digitized. The conservator is retained for consultation throughout the project.

- Equipment and software are ordered/received, then transported, set up and tested at the new digitization lab in St. Augustine at Government House (Caswell; Renner; IT staff)
- Candidates for project staff (project manager, TBD; and programmer, TBD) are recruited, interviewed, and hired by September 30, 2012 (Caswell; Cusick; Nemmers; Renner). (Caswell et al., 2011: 14)

This next narrative work plan version was used to accommodate an online textbox format with a limited number of words. Due to space limitations, those responsible for leading project activities were excluded from the narrative.

July 2011—Project preparation and planning, contract with CAPS for evaluation component, secure IRB approval, create a marketing campaign to include a promotional "gimmick" to attract undergrad and grad students to participate. **August–September**—Advertise, hire and train graduate student with computer science experience; build an inventory of supplies; build the website. **October–April**—Facilitate six Collaborating with Strangers sessions and follow-up to each by posting participants' information online for a limited time frame so that participants can read everyone's information sheets and find possible ideas for sharing resources, mentoring, or for collaboration. Two sessions will be facilitated during the Fall semester in the first floor study area at Library West next to Starbucks; two during January/February and two during March/April, to be scheduled in the Marston Science Library and the University Gallery. Throughout the time period, participants who post their CoLAB ideas for sharing resources, mentoring, or collaboration to the webpage will compete for $300 micro grants to support winning creative partnership efforts. Awards will be judged by representatives from Fine Arts, Science and Engineering. **May–June**—Complete final evaluation and report; write article to submit to scholarly publications, and Libraries' newsletter; submit a poster to be presented at state and national library organizations; and add article, videos and documentation to the IR@UF. (Clapp et al., 2011: 3)

A table format allows for the conveyance of much information while remaining in a compact container (see table 6.1). This format permits a reviewer greater capacity to visualize the project time frame, activities, and participants carrying out the various activities. Another example of table format was used to illustrate a fictitious mini-grant project described in chapter 3.

Table 6.2 demonstrates a simple chart format excluding information about those responsible for leading or executing the activities noted in the chart. This small research project was managed by a librarian with support from a student assistant.

The next example of a plan of work and timeline includes budget information for contributed effort and costs (which was information requested by the sponsor) for personnel and supplies. It provides reviewers with information about how and when resources will be allocated and spent to complete the various planned activities.

Month 1	Order conservation and imaging supplies ($14,651) plus 5% head of Conservation over two years ($6,784)
	Sort collection by type and size, and establish triage schedule.

Table 6.1. Excerpt of a Work Plan in a Table Format

TIME FRAME	ACTIVITY	PERSONS RESPONSIBLE
March, 2015	• Hire Student Assistant • Develop full title list of books written by women for children in sciences (1790–1890) • Cataloging report/spreadsheet • Narrow spreadsheet of possible candidates for inclusion	Alteri, Curator Student Asst./Alteri Van Kleeck, Cataloger Student Assistant
April–May, 2015	• Selection criteria • Selection of titles • WorldCat training for Student Assistant • Review of materials for scarcity • Develop final list of 200 titles (incorporating comparative editions)	Alteri Alteri/Student Assist. Alteri Student Assistant Alteri
May–June, 2015	• Check all bibliographic data to make sure it matches with the material in hand	Student Assistant
July–December, 2015	• Research on general time period and cultural significance • Research on specific titles and authors • Design format of bibliography • Type all titles with bibliographic data into the Bibliography template • Meet with consultant	Alteri/Student Assist. Student Assistant Student Assistant Student Assistant Student Assistant Alteri/Rauch
January–July, 2016	• Write all annotations for items included in annotated bibliography, note when there are multiple editions of the same title • Meet with consultant	Alteri/ Student Assist. Alteri/Rauch
August–October, 2016	• Proofread annotated bibliography for content and grammatical mistakes	Alteri/Rauch/Van Kleeck
November, 2016	• Upload finished product in UFDC	Alteri/ UF Digital Production Services

(Alteri, Rauch, and de Farber, 2014: 9)

Month 2   Hire and train conservation assistant ($1,795 for 150 hours each year).
           Begin treating #1–50.

Month 3–4 Initial treatment of items #1–50.
           Hire and train imaging assistant ($3,960 for 330 hours each year).
           Transfer #1–50 to Digital Library Center (DLC) for imaging preservation.

Month 5–6 Initial treatment of items #51–100.
           Return of #1–50 from DLC. Complete conservation and re-shelve.
           Transfer #51–100 to DLC.

(Nemmers and de Farber, 2009: 5)

Table 6.2. Excerpt of a Work Plan in a Table Format Excluding Personnel Information

TIME FRAME	PLANNED ACTIVITIES
July–August 2010	Recruit library school student (Florida State University or University of South Florida) for two semester internship to gather the contact information for the surveys, assist with the compilation of the results, and examine the job ads
September–December 2010	Conduct literature review Surveys (identify random samples, collect contact information, develop questions, obtain institutional approval for human subject research)
January 2011	Submit 6 month report
February 2011–May 2011	Distribute surveys and compile results Record and analyze data from job ads
June 2011	Present findings at 2011 ALA Annual Conference

(Simpson, 2009: 3)

Table 6.3. Excerpt of a Work Plan in a Gantt Chart Format Excluding Personnel Information

TIMETABLE	QUARTER 1			QUARTER 2			QUARTER 3			QUARTER 4		
	OCT	NOV	DEC	JAN	FEB	MAR	APRIL	MAY	JUNE	JULY	AUG	SEPT
1. Purchase equipment, software, servers, and aerial photography	■	■										
2. Hire and train students techs	▨	▨	▨									
3. Install and configure new GIS virtual server and open access server expansion		■	■	■								
4. Digitize 1971–1990 aerial photographs and paper indexes / Convert FDOT files to archivable and accessible format	▨	▨	▨	▨	▨	▨						

(McAuliffe, de Farber, and Haas, 2009: 8)

Table 6.3 illustrates the use of a Gantt chart format without providing specific information about those responsible for leading activities. This version helps to facilitate a reviewer's process of evaluating the viability of a time-consuming and labor-intensive project.

⑥ Prepare a Grant Application Budget

Once the work plan is more or less complete, the next component to prepare, logically, is the budget. The purpose of the budget is to demonstrate to the reviewer that the resources needed to fuel the project have been articulated completely and reasonably. These resources include both the cash amounts being requested from the sponsor, and in-kind contributions (also referred to as cost share) provided by the applicant organization, project team members, the applicant organization, and/or its partners.

Budgets essentially tell the truth about the intent of the project, regardless of the narrative content. How the project team intends to spend its awarded funds speaks volumes about the team's management and planning capacity. Experienced reviewers will check the budget prior to reviewing anything else in the proposal package. For instance, a budget can reveal whether the project offers a new answer to a problem or opportunity. Or, it can share the story of a library project that has been floundering and needs to be resuscitated through new marketing approaches. Inflated budgets include unnecessary budget requests such as for additional staff or equipment that appear to be excessive. And budgets can provide hints that the project will move forward regardless of the outcome of the reviewers' decisions.

Most sponsors provide budget forms within the guidelines; otherwise, applicants must create their own budget presentation format. When provided by the sponsor, these forms are intended to create uniformity across all applicants so reviewers can easily find the information they need throughout the review process. Library accountants generally are comfortable completing grant application budget forms if they understand the project activities and have thoroughly read the sponsor's instructions that define expense categories and describe how to complete the forms. Online forms sometimes include embedded formulas that further ease the entry process and ensure that calculations are accurate.

To prepare the budget, the project team should coordinate its planning by using the work plan content as a guide for decision making. It will not be difficult for the team to discern where grant resources will be needed to complete activities and steps. If in-kind contributions are planned to be included in the budget document—because of matching requirements or voluntarily to make a project competitive—then a list of all personnel who plan to work on the various steps of the work plan should be created. With support from these personnel and supervisors, the next step is to coordinate with the library's accountant to create a spreadsheet with embedded formulas that allow for the manipulation of percent of effort. The formulas should generate the respective amount of salary and benefits costs associated with the anticipated percentage of time a library employee plans to contribute during the grant period.

If the project leader plans to recover salary/benefits costs of a current library staff member's time, then the percentage to be included in the cash request should be calculated in the same way described above. In these cases, the budget narrative should include a statement indicating that funds received from the sponsor (for a current library employee) will be used to hire part-time or student workers to manage the workload while the library employee is occupied by the grant-funded project. Some sponsors avoid awarding funds to replace salaries and benefits costs for existing full-time employees.

The work plan also will provide ideas for other types of expenses that will be required to complete the project. Temporary time-limited employees—also referred to as outside professional services (OPS)—consultants, travel, supplies, equipment, and other expenses may be necessary. All expense categories such as these should be allowable as verified in the guidelines. Correctly estimating the costs of these types of expenses may well be the difference between an award and a declination. Some reviewers will scrutinize expenses for padding of any type. If it appears that an applicant has guessed or inflated travel, equipment, or consulting fees in comparison to the stated work or results anticipated through this expense, then it should be expected that this issue will be discussed during review deliberations. When reviewers talk about such things, the quality of review scores usually suffers.

Guidelines often state a requirement for including detailed budgets, and some also want to see a budget summary form for projects requiring more than one year to complete. Applicants must share information about how each expense amount has been calculated. For OPS, the detailed budget should indicate plans to hire a temporary employee by including the number of hours per week (or month), multiplied by the number of weeks (or months), and multiplied by the hourly wage planned for this position. The detailed budget will include the formula used to determine the total amount to be spent for a part-time, temporary employee. If fringe benefits will be applied, then the percentage used to make this calculation should be included in the budget detail.

Expenses related to consultants often require the inclusion of an hourly or daily fee with accompanying number of hours or days of work expected to be performed. This can be tricky if the arrangement is to compensate a consultant with a flat fee. If this is the case, it is best to request that the consultant estimate the number of days or hours required to complete the agreed-upon responsibilities. Vendors also can be considered consultants or "other services." These include those who plan to provide digitization, microfilming, or external conservation services as part of the project.

For travel expenses, the application should include round-trip estimates for coach airfare, ground transportation, and per diem food allowances that meet the applicant organization's typical reimbursement policies. Most sponsors want to know departure and arrival locations if this is known. If travel will be conducted by car, then round-trip miles should be determined and mileage expenses calculated based on the applicant organization's travel policies.

Supplies and equipment can pose different challenges. For government grant applications, it is best to exclude requested funds or in-kind contributions for supplies. Tracking the use and accompanying cost of general office supplies for a specific project is virtually impossible. If the supplies are intended for specific conservation of documents, photographs, and books within the project scope, then these are examples of expenses that can be tracked, as they are specialized in nature. For academic library applicants, typically "supplies" are defined as items each costing less than $5,000. Although computers and other electronic devices generally might be considered to be "equipment" in other contexts, they may not meet the minimum expense amount required to qualify as entries in the equipment category, per a university's accounting policies. In these cases, each computer would be detailed in the supplies expense category. Estimates for supplies and equipment should be obtained through written vendor estimates or online retail sources.

The "other" expense category is often included as a budget category. Sometimes vendor expenses are included here. Furniture and items that otherwise do not fit in any of the categories previously mentioned will be included in "other."

The project team may decide to include other types of in-kind contributions beyond librarian and library staff effort. Determining the cost associated with other contributions poses a challenge. Renting a venue may be considered an acceptable in-kind contribution if the venue has an existing rental fee schedule. A printing vendor may agree to contribute services, and this also is acceptable. Volunteer (nonemployee) staff time can be included if the applicant can document the determination of the hourly rate attributed to the type of tasks being performed by volunteers. A possible source for determining how to value volunteer time might be an accountant in your county's or city's parks and recreation department, or any government or nonprofit agency that manages a large number of volunteers. Generally, if an expense can be tracked or documented, then it can be included in the budget. If partnering organizations plan to give in-kind contributions toward the project budget, then these contributions must be documented by letters of commitment within the application, and then verified through subsequent correspondence during the post-award reporting period.

The last budget category typically found in government sponsor budget forms is indirect cost (IDC). IDC represents costs related to an organization's overhead expenses. Most federal sponsors allow for IDC expenses to be included in a grant application budget. Librarians working in academic libraries should obtain a copy of the university's Federally Negotiated Indirect Cost Rate Agreement, which outlines specific percentages to be charged for research projects, teaching, training, or other types of sponsored activities. Projects related to academic libraries are usually categorized as "other sponsored activities" and carry the lowest percentage rate of overhead costs. If the total direct costs are $50,000 (excluding in-kind contributions), and the IDC rate for this type of project is 30 percent, according to the rate agreement, then the total direct and indirect cost will be $65,000 (this would be the total grant application request).

For academic librarians, if including IDC in the budget is allowable, based on a sponsor's guidelines, then IDC is calculated as a percentage of the direct project costs and must be combined with director costs to achieve the total project cost. Librarians can contact university or college grants administrators to determine whether a waiver of including IDC within the budget is possible. For public or private libraries, it is best to use 10 percent as the applicable IDC rate. Ten percent is a reasonable amount. Anything higher than this percentage may generate a red flag by reviewers. Examples of grant application budget formats can be found in the University of Florida's Institutional Repository (http://ufdc.ufl.edu/irgrants) as components of submitted and/or awarded grant applications.

Prepare the Opening Paragraph

The opening paragraph should contain answers to these questions:

- What is the name of the applicant?
- What organization(s) is the applicant collaborating with?
- How much money is the applicant requesting, and how much is contributed cost share?
- What is the title of the project?

- What does the project plan to achieve?
- How long will the project take to complete?

Using this formula will remove much of the guesswork in trying to determine how to start a proposal summary or a narrative. And, it is applicable to any application.

Why is this formula effective in introducing a reviewer to a project? Reviewers want to know what project they are reading about, and how much is being requested, right from the start of the application. Having to spend additional time searching an application for the answers to basic questions inadvertently can create additional work for reviewers.

The following examples illustrate the use of this formula in the opening narrative paragraph. Often the same paragraph is used for the abstract or paragraph summary. The first example goes beyond the formula to justify inclusion of the University of Puerto Rico as its collaborating partner. It also discloses the difference in the quality of microfilm available from each institution, while bolstering the applicant's credibility. Other examples can be found in chapter 3.

> The University of Florida (UF) in partnership with the University of Puerto Rico (UPR) requests $343,850 (with $106,984 in combined contributed cost share from both institutions) to select, digitize and make available to the Library of Congress 100,000 newspaper pages through the *National Digital Newspaper Project* (NDNP). Approximately half of the pages will come from historic Florida papers (1836–1922) and the remaining half from newspapers published in Puerto Rico (1836–1922). The project builds on previous NEH/NDNP newspaper digitization grant awards received by the George A. Smathers Libraries at UF and NEH funding for microfilming Puerto Rico newspapers received by UPR-Rio Piedras Campus (UPR-RP). The long history (since 1930) of the connection between the Latin American Collection at Smathers Libraries and the Caribbean makes possible the cooperation between UF and the UPR-RP in this project. Previous successful cooperative work performed by UF and UPR with government documents projects, the Digital Library of the Caribbean (dLOC), and most recently the digitization of the newspaper *El Mundo* (issues from 1928, 1938, and 1939) provides a sound foundation for this expanded project. Although Puerto Rico newspapers are preserved on master microfilm, it should be noted that the vast majority of historical newspaper microfilming in Florida was performed by UF beginning in the 1940s. UF has the largest and most complete set of newspaper microfilm in the state. (Reakes et al., 2012: 1)

The second example presents an excerpt from a longer opening paragraph that expresses arguments for supporting the applicant's strengths and assets, and makes a case for why funding of the project is important within the applicant's current situation.

> The George A. Smathers Libraries (Libraries) at the University of Florida (UF) requests NEH support of $500,000 to match $1.5 million to be raised in the next four years to endow acquisitions, public and scholarly outreach activities, and collaborative digitization projects related to the Jewish experience in Florida, Latin America, and the Caribbean. Florida, sometimes referred to as the New Ellis Island and the Gateway to the Americas, is located at the crossroads for trade and migrating populations. As such it has played a pivotal role, within this hemisphere, in developing an inseparable history and culture highlighted by the diversity of those who adopted Florida or simply passed through its borders. UF is uniquely qualified to lead a national and international effort to inspire greater study of the Jewish diaspora and the ways in which minority groups and individuals contribute to the wider society, and as such plays a pivotal role in mapping the diversity of histories and cultures in this hemisphere. (Jefferson et al., 2014: 7)

ⓖ Create the Grant Project Title

A good project title is a valuable commodity. The project title serves to remind reviewers of the core project intent. Reviewers typically receive a list of all the applicant names with respective application titles and requested grant amounts to organize the review process. A title may often be the only piece of information readily accessible to a reviewer during the finalization of scores. Essentially, the goal of a title is to convey the project in such a way as to most fully and instantly inform or remind the reviewer about the proposed project content.

These are the characteristics of an effective title. The title

1. generates a mental picture of the project;
2. is memorable and compels the reviewer to want to read the application;
3. is easy to say and read;
4. can be abbreviated, if necessary; and
5. conveys active engagement, a solution, or a result.

Examples of grant project titles that illustrate the desired characteristics include:

- "Library Technobus: A Computer Lab on Wheels"
- "Libraries as Hip-Hop Techspace"
- "A Network of Makerspaces in Libraries: An Opportunity to Transform Libraries into Centers of Creativity and Innovation through Making"
- "3D Printed Children's Books for Blind Children"

These project titles were submitted by applicants to the 2014 Knight News Challenge funded by the Knight Foundation to applicants of the giving program titled "How Might We Leverage Libraries as a Platform to Build More Knowledgeable Communities?" (Knight Foundation, 2015).

Consider a scenario where a reviewer has read and evaluated thirty proposal packages. At the review session where review panelists gather to determine awards and declinations, each reviewer wants to perform his or her role well. This means being able to discuss the attributes and weaknesses of all the proposals. A reviewer might refer to an application several times during these deliberations. He or she may use the name of the applicant organization as a means for identifying the proposal being discussed. But, if the title of the discussed project is well crafted, easily remembered, and evocative, then reviewers might opt to use the title as a reference point instead. This, of course, is the best option for the applicant. Every time the title is included in the discussion, it begins to come to life with an identity. When it comes to grant-seeking, the project title can be a game changer.

ⓖ Prepare a Project Description

After completing the above components, it is time to write the project description. Unlike the project work plan, this is always a narrative section and reflects what the project team wants to achieve during the grant period (beginning and end of the funded project). The project description serves to present the full concept of the project.

Sponsors do not consistently request a project description narrative; rather, the guidelines may request other section headings such as "Project Significance," "Project Need to Be Addressed," or "Project Impact." Librarians preparing this content face the challenge of determining where to write about the actual project description. Including the opening paragraph content, as described previously, regardless of whether the sponsor requests this or not, helps to mitigate the situation when a project description is omitted by the sponsor. Ultimately, you should find the best place within the first page of the narrative to insert project description content. Otherwise, the reviewer will have to spend extra time determining exactly what is included within the scope of the project.

The project description should answer the following questions, which also are typically found in proposal guidelines:

- What are the goal and objectives of the project?
- What will be the benefits of the project, and who will be its beneficiaries?
- How will the objectives or strategies be carried out and by whom?
- Where will the project take place?

Although these questions appear to be simple to answer, they are frequently misunderstood. In the context of a project description, the applicant should describe the overarching achievement the project will strive to actualize. It is usually one concept. In the process of reaching this end, a project team may execute several smaller strategies and activities. These will result in the achievement of objectives that together provide benefits to various constituents while the team is actively in the process of reaching the ultimate goal.

Using the SMART goal development method works best for grant proposals, especially in describing a grant project. This mnemonic acronym means that the goal and objectives should be specific, measurable, assignable, realistic, and time related (Doran, 1981). Examples of various project descriptions can be found in chapter 3.

For instance, if the project will result in new collaborations for infusing technology into a variety of humanities courses, then this will be the goal of the project. On its journey to achieve this end, the project team plans to complete a series of project strategies, such as:

- Establish an advisory group to select participants and content.
- Design and present an intensive boot camp–style training conference for invited participants.
- Secure digital humanities trainers with noted expertise in digital curation, geo-referencing, and related activities.
- Design and execute an evaluation process. (Taylor et al., 2015)

Working backward from these strategies, the project team can generate its project objectives to:

- Serve sixty invited participants representing a wide variety of humanities disciplines, as determined by an advisory council.
- Secure four respected trainers to validate the quality of planned workshops, with expertise in digital curation, georeferencing, and related activities, as determined by an advisory council.

- Present hands-on, practical experiences within a two-day training conference, featuring small-group sessions to maximize learning and development of collaborative relationships.
- Gather a three-minute video from each participant that describes their experiences related to the themes of sessions one month after boot camp completion, answering questions related to plans for using digital humanities activities within humanities courses. (Taylor et al., 2015)

The goal of the project combined with the project objectives can form the foundation for the project description. To complete the section, you can include descriptions of audiences or patrons who will be served by the project, the benefits each type of population served will experience, and benefits that will be achieved for those collaborating in the project or for the library applicant itself.

⑥ Request Letters of Commitment and Support

At this point in the proposal development process, the project team has completed draft components including the work plan, budget, opening paragraph, title, and project description. If it hasn't already done so, the project team is now prepared to invite those external to the applicant library to commit to participating in the project or to simply provide an endorsement of the project.

As described in chapter 3 for mini-grant applications, letters of commitment serve to verify the commitment and type of involvement by those outside a library's project team. Some guidelines require submission of these letters from project team members as well.

E-MAIL MESSAGE TEMPLATE
FOR REQUESTING A LETTER OF COMMITMENT

Thank you for agreeing to participate in the project, [include working title]. I am writing to formally request a letter of commitment to participate in the project as we have discussed. The letter should include your letterhead, and be addressed as follows:

- Name of project director or sponsor program officer
- Title
- Address
- [Opening] "I am writing to confirm my commitment and participation for the proposed project, [insert title]." Indicate agreement to serve in specific role(s) and describe these.
- [Body] Describe your expertise and respond to these questions:
  - Why is the project important to you in relation to your field of expertise and interest?
  - Why is it important to the field, and/or to others (share information about those who will benefit and how)?
- [Closing] Include a statement of endorsement and signature.

Reviewers will look for letters of commitment that authentically confirm project participation by authors who are external to the applicant library. For this reason, it is best not to create draft letters for letter authors. Instead, providing a prospective letter author with an e-mail message outlining the project specifics, a series of questions about the author's future role or organization's role in completing the project, as well as the author's view of the project's importance, and instructions on how and by when to send the letter, usually produces the desired results.

The textbox on page 111 is a template of an e-mail message requesting a letter of commitment.

Requesting letters of support should be viewed as a separate activity. These letters are similar to letters of commitment, but exclude statements describing the role or responsibilities the author will perform to complete the project. Instead, support letters should be written by those external to the applicant organization, and by those who are not performing any role in the project. Letters written by employees of the applicant organization for the author's signature are generally considered to be weaker than those authored by experts outside the applicant organization. Reviewers consider letters of support that originate from the applicant institution to be self-promoting rather than objective. Regardless, authors of support letters should be experts in a field related to the project in order to provide credible rationale for its importance, and justification for being funded. Because of these distinctions, librarians should be cautious when requesting letters—either letters of commitment (which should include project support) or letters of support (which are offered in the application to articulate an objective third party project statement of project significance or endorsement).

◎ Prepare a Statement of Significance and/or Need to Be Addressed

A challenging component of any application, especially for organizations in the humanities, is the statement of significance. A needs statement may be a required component, within the narrative section, to accompany the statement of significance, or it is sometimes required as an individual narrative section.

What is a statement of significance and/or need? This narrative section is an opportunity to educate the reader about the values of a proposed project. Essentially, this narrative section should answer these sample questions:

- Why is this project important?
- What has the project team done to study it or to build the service, program, or collection being proposed?
- Who else has studied it, used it, or contributed to its development; and what have they learned?
- Who will be interested or benefit from the project's results in the future?
- What else can be learned by executing the project?
- How and where did the project importance or need develop or evolve?
- What exactly is the gap, need, or problem that inspired the project?
- How does the project support or relate to the field or other fields?
- How is the project different from other attempts or projects developed in the past to address these issues?
- What impact will the project have?

Sponsors want information that justifies the investment of their funds to improve a situation, solve a problem, broaden impact, or fill a need. These statements should provide information in the form of evidence supporting the applicant's project goals and objectives. The sponsor may provide instructions within the guidelines to assist applicants in determining how to present information about significance and need. Guidelines also may contain evaluation criteria related to how the sponsor plans to judge the merits of statements of significance and need.

How does an applicant provide evidence of significance and need in order for a project to be considered worthy? Using some of the questions listed previously provides a starting point for establishing a container for this type of information. Next, determine the content available at hand, such as documentation related to work previously performed by members of the project team. A literature review may yield resources that describe previous research, projects, issue analysis, or attempts by others to move forward or solve problems related to the proposed project's goals and objectives.

Librarians characteristically have skills to find evidence that supports an idea, solution, or need. Significance and needs narrative sections benefit greatly from the contributions of librarians, especially when pooled to collaboratively tackle this task. To home in on this assignment, librarians can use this question as a departure point: What questions can the project team answer to articulate the value of the project in ways that will engage the reader into wanting to learn more? Hooking the reader's interest at the start of a proposal, with evidence-based information, will make the difference between inspiring a review of the entire proposal at one sitting, or causing the reviewer to read part of the proposal with interest and the remainder as an obligation. An example of a statement of significance is included in appendix 6.1.

Prepare a Project Dissemination Plan

The purpose of the project dissemination plan is to provide reviewers with a description of the activities conceived by the project team to ensure that the project will be broadly communicated and promoted. This section of the narrative presents evidence of the project team's existing networks, routine methods for distributing media releases, and capacity for promoting aspects of the project, including the initial grant award announcement. As a general practice, most sponsors want their grantees to promote the (1) notification of a grant award, (2) events or activities related to the project, and (3) results achieved or outputs produced by way of the project and award. Some foundation sponsors, however, prefer to remain anonymous and are not interested in promoting awards. The award notification and administration documents will provide grantees with provisions for acknowledging the sponsor.

A librarian leading a project team should seek details about the library's standard procedures for publicizing and promoting projects, workshops, outreach, achievements, or other library news topics. These may include the production and distribution of news releases, posters, online links embedded on the library's home page and blog, and Facebook and listserv postings. Interviewing those in the library responsible for public relations and communications will provide valuable details for possible inclusion in the application narrative.

Beyond these examples, the project team can search for appropriate conferences or symposia to which they would propose presentations related to awarded grants. The timing of such opportunities should be considered vis-à-vis the project grant period. Presentations occurring too close to the start of the project, unless intended to promote subsequent participation in the project in some way, should occur within the last quarter of the grant period. This provides a means for disseminating the project's results, lessons learned, and best practices. Offering a list of three possible conferences within the dissemination plan provides reviewers with a sense that the project team has done its homework.

The project team should identify conference presentation opportunities that have yet to be determined and those for which the applicant has not missed the deadline for submission of a presentation idea. Better yet, members of the project team can build credibility if a project presentation—appropriate for disseminating aspects of activities that are precursors to the proposed project—has already been approved, and can be listed as such in the dissemination plan. Those conferences to be held in proximity to the applicant organization or its partnering organizations also are good candidates for building a realistic dissemination plan.

If presenting at conferences is included in the dissemination plan, then the travel also should be included in the budget. Some libraries provide travel funding for librarians and staff to present at conferences. If this is the case, then the budget can include travel funding as an in-kind contribution. Budgeting travel expenses can be tricky, especially when the conference sponsor has yet to disclose its details. A lack of information such as conference location, hotel, cost of a room night, and exact dates can cause accountants to determine a best-guess scenario that can be used to estimate the conference travel costs. Common practice is to use estimates based on the previous year's actual conference fees and location. Reviewers will understand the nature of these estimated costs, and librarians should not exclude travel costs because of a lack of information. If the project is awarded and the travel estimate is more or less than estimated, then a budget change request, if necessary, can be submitted to the sponsor during the post-award period.

Other ways of disseminating a project include events and meetings hosted by the library and its partners, videos posted to YouTube describing the project and its results, and posting instructional tutorials or presenting webinars about project innovations or lessons learned that are replicable. And dissemination opportunities through social media generated by a project's audiences and participants can show reviewers the extent to which the team has considered these types of promotional avenues. Creating project web pages and linking strategies that point to a website's project results should be included, as well as possible plans for search engine optimization, including a *Wikipedia* presence, are other options. Regardless, librarians have no shortage of ways to promote projects, which makes the dissemination narrative section an obvious opportunity to shine. An example of a dissemination plan is provided below.

> *Unearthing St. Augustine* will be promoted broadly to local, national and international scholars, teachers and the general public. The City of St. Augustine and the state of Florida anniversaries in 2013 and 2015 respectively will provide the most beneficial opportunities for promoting this project, its partners and its outcomes. UF and its partners will create and widely disseminate information about the project and its resources. UF will publish project technical documentation and publicize system architecture and subsequently released as open source programming. To increase discovery of and access to St. Augustine resources, UF will contribute digital objects and metadata to digital repositories and collections. UF digital collections are automatically disseminated via OAI

and MARCXML feeds to multiple harvesters and repositories including: Trove, NINES, 18thConnect, WorldCat, OAIster, and other aggregators.

UF Libraries public information office will provide professional promotional and marketing services to implement many of the publicity strategies. Collection managers and subject specialists at UF and partner St. Augustine institutions will promote the new resource to researchers and colleagues. Additional publicity will be conducted using:

- Press releases to media outlets and listservs, both general and subject-specific
- Articles published in journals, newsletters, and blogs
- Presentations at conferences and meetings
- Contributions of digital objects to social networking sites to encourage discovery

The strength of the dissemination plan is that Advisors will use their extensive network of international colleagues to disseminate information about and encourage future development of the interactive digital portal. As leading experts in the archaeology, historic preservation and history of Florida and colonial America, the Advisors will effectively and authoritatively promote the project to a very broad audience. Their efforts, along with publicity efforts undertaken by UF and its partners, will ensure that the project receives the widest exposure. (Caswell et. al., 2011: 20)

⑥ Prepare the Evaluation Plan

Any grant activity or anticipated result can be evaluated, and this likely will be the attitude of proposal reviewers. A thoughtful plan for evaluation within a grant proposal narrative delivers the strongest impression of an applicant's competence. Furthermore, it speaks volumes about the degree of commitment with which the project team plans to execute the project's proposed activities and use the evaluation results for future decision making and planning.

Sponsors usually require an evaluation plan, and if they do not, the project team should consider including one regardless. Ways to quantitatively and qualitatively evaluate a project or aspects of a project and its results vary widely. Sometimes a simple paragraph description will suffice—it depends on the individual sponsor's reviewers' expectations.

Over the past twenty years, the outcomes measurement method, which uses a logic model template popularized largely by United Way agencies and adopted by other sponsor agencies and foundations in the United States, has become a format commonly used by many sponsor agencies including those funding libraries. Any type of activity or result can be accommodated within a typical evaluation logic model framework.

A logic model template generally includes space to document a project's anticipated inputs (resources), activities, outputs, anticipated outcomes and impacts, and indicators and methods or sources for measuring outcomes and impacts. Table 6.4 shows an example. Using such a template can help the project team plan specific aspects of the project that may not have been revealed while the team was designing the work plan—so updating the work plan to include evaluation activities should not be overlooked.

The important question the project team should address in the proposal is: How will the project team determine whether the project achieved success or a degree of success? The team is essentially predicting the future by defining the project's success. Defining success, or as Stephen Covey states in his habit number two: "Begin with the end in mind is based on the principle that all things are created twice. There's a mental first creation,

Table 6.4. Excerpt from Evaluation Plan Using a Logic Model Format

RESOURCES	ACTIVITIES	OUTPUTS	OUTCOMES	INDICATORS	SOURCES/METHODS
127 reels of microfilm: The *Jewish Floridian*, 1928–1990 Vendors: Backstage Library Works; Creekside Digital Staff: George A. Smathers Libraries' project technicians	Microfilm converted to digital format by Creekside Digital Digital images of the *Jewish Floridian* are ingested and processed by the UF Digital Library Center Creation of collection website, instructional and promotional materials and provision of instruction	# Digital newspaper files and metadata: the *Jewish Floridian*, 1928–1990 1 landing page for collection, including narrative 1 permanent URL to send to partner websites 3 instructional presentations to partner institutions 1 tutorial video	1. The targeted population uses information or services that were not previously available.	1. Significant increase in the number of views of and visits to the Florida Digital Newspaper Library (FDNL)	1. UF system generated statistics for the use of the FDNL /UF system generated statistics to be gathered when the *Jewish Floridian* collection is first available; statistics generated 6 months after collection is launched
Partners: Jewish Museum of Florida, three public library systems			2. The targeted population uses technology to get information.	2. 2,000 views of the *Jewish Floridian* digital collection within 6 months of completion (March 30, 2014)	2. UF system generated statistics for the *Jewish Floridian* views and visits

(Jefferson and de Farber, 2012: 29–30)

Table 6.5. Excerpt from Evaluation Plan Focused on Goals, Quantitative and Qualitative Data Gathering

OBJECTIVES/QUESTIONS	INFORMATION REQUIRED	INFORMATION SOURCE	METHOD TO COLLECT INFORMATION	RESPONSIBLE PARTY
Objective 2: Raising visibility of and improving access to relevant UF research				
How much money was spent to help researchers publish results of women's health or sex/gender differences studies in open access journals?	Expenditure data including expenditure reports	OA administrators	Data mining from appropriate sources including the OA collaborators	Team
How many articles were published using the open access funds?	Expenditure data including expenditure reports	OA administrators	Data mining from appropriate sources including the OA collaborators	Team
What are the researchers perceptions of the open access publishing fund and/or publishing in open access journals? For instance, did they find relevant OA journals to publish in? What did they know about open access prior to the funding? Were they satisfied with the application process? How important was getting the funding to their ability to publish in open access journals?	Researchers' perceptions	Researchers who received open access funding	Survey	Professional Evaluator

(Tennant et al., 2013: 11)

and a physical or second creation of things. . . . The carpenter's rule is 'measure twice, cut once.' You have to make sure that the blueprint, the first creation, is really what you want, that you have thought everything through" (Covey, 2004: 99).

How a project will be evaluated is an essential topic for all project teams to address. Quantitatively, this can be achieved by positing the number of projected participants who might be expected to attend a planned workshop or lecture, the number of pages or books or linear feet to be digitized, the number of new cataloging records that will be created, the number of hours volunteers will provide to improve literacy in a community, or the number of visitors who will use a new web resource.

Qualitative assessment provides new challenges. These evaluation methods focus on answering open questions such as:

- How did the project impact participants?
- What learning was achieved?
- For what purposes have participants used the new resource?
- What was the most important component of the workshop, resource, or service, and why?
- How will the activity/service/resource enhance your future library experiences?

The challenge for the project team will be to devise strategies for obtaining information from project beneficiaries. Methods may include interviews by a neutral interviewer, surveys, or focus groups led by a neutral facilitator. Table 6.5 illustrates a project team's plan for evaluating a project.

ⓖ Prepare the Abstract or Project Summary

Although the abstract or project summary usually appears at the front of an application package, it should be one of the last sections you prepare. This gives the project team the opportunity to hone every sentence, achieving the most concise information that highlights the key and unique aspects of the project. The purpose of the abstract is to give reviewers the most complete snapshot of the project. It helps them to capture the essence of the project idea and strategies for its completion when they first read the proposal. And it gives them a quick place to find the detailed information they need to argue for the proposal's merits or its weaknesses, during the review panel's deliberations.

Content of the abstract varies depending on the sponsor's guidelines. Regardless, a good way to start is to cut and paste the project narrative's opening paragraph, to create the first paragraph of the abstract. An abstract should include the project's primary goal and objectives as shared in the narrative. If the abstract is one page in length, then you have plenty of space to pull out the highlights of the project that you have included throughout the different narrative sections. An abstract is a place to take credit for innovative aspects of the project, unusual or outstanding benefits the project will generate, unique partnerships or audiences to be served, and plans for future sustainability of project activities.

Answers to the following questions often are included in an abstract:

- What is the proposed project goal and objectives?
- How much is the applicant requesting?
- Who will the project serve?
- What are the project's expected outcomes or products?

This is an example of a short paragraph abstract for submission within an online application container with delimited characters:

The George A. Smathers Libraries at the University of Florida (UF) respectfully request $4,292 to promote and facilitate five Collaborating with Strangers (CoLAB) networking workshops to connect 250 College of Journalism and Communications students, staff and faculty with others from business, engineering and health sciences colleges. Based on successful pilot workshops using the CoLAB Planning Series® facilitation methods, participants will engage in 3-minute conversations with "strangers" on topics related to research, passions, skills and other "hidden" assets. An average of 50 participants per session will meet 12–20 strangers resulting in 5,000 possible total connections. The project goal is to use proven facilitation processes and online follow-up to eliminate networking barriers, while creating the fertile ground for creative, entrepreneurial ideas that arise from focused conversations between those in and outside the field of mass communications. (Hines and de Farber, 2011: 2)

⑥ Prepare Key Personnel Information

Providing evidence that project team members and partner organization contributors are qualified to carry out the project to a successful outcome assists reviewers in determining the degree to which projects are feasible or sustainable. This can be achieved by preparing short biographical paragraphs containing the following information:

- Full name and position title, employer organization name
- Designation if serving as the project director, or codirector; or in academic terms, principal investigator (PI) or coprincipal investigator (co-PI)
- Percent of effort contributed as cost share or to be recovered through requested funds from sponsor
- Brief biographical information and current responsibilities
- Role expected to be performed during the project's grant period

The following excerpt provides an example of how to prepare a description of a project team member or collaborating contributor.

Patrick Reakes—(Principal Investigator—two years at 10% FTE cost share) is the Chair of the Humanities & Social Sciences Library [and] previously served as Chair of Departmental Libraries for two years and Head of the Neuharth Journalism Library at UF for nine years. He holds an MSLS from Florida State University (FSU), a BS in Public Relations from UF, and is a graduate of the General Motors Management Development School. He was recently a Fellow in the Association of Research Libraries (ARL) Research Library Leadership Program, a highly competitive executive leadership program designed and sponsored by ARL member libraries to facilitate the development of future senior-level leaders in large research libraries. Prior to coming to UF, he served as a law librarian at Florida Coastal School of Law, where he headed the interlibrary loan department and served as adjunct faculty member. He has been a reference and instruction librarian at FSU, where he served as the Business Librarian. His current research focus is on the impacts of the evolving digital environment on news research and archiving.

Role: Provide general project direction, liaison with the Library of Congress, serve as lead vendor contact and assist the Project Coordinator with coordinating internal library staff in all other areas of production. (Reakes et al., 2012: 16)

⑥ Prepare a Budget Justification or Budget Narrative

A budget justification, budget notes, or budget narrative provides reviewers with information that is not available within the actual budget form and that generates confidence in the manner in which the budget was created. It also describes why the expense item or cost is necessary to successfully actualize the project. Although detailed calculations may appear in the budget detail, these details are insufficient to explain the purpose of the expense for achieving anticipated project results, or to reveal more specifics about how funds will be spent in order to undertake the particular activities outlined in the project description or work plan. The budget justification should include narrative and detailed calculations for all cash requests and in-kind contribution expense categories, as well as other cash and its source(s) planned to match the sponsored request. For vendor services or equipment expenses, the source of these estimates should be identified here, whether a website or written estimate. If the written estimate is the source, then a copy should be included in the appendixes. The indirect costs (IDC) rate assigned to this type of project, and a calculation of how the rate was applied to project expenses, also should be included in this document. An example of a budget narrative is shown in appendix 6.2.

⑥ Prepare the Appendixes

The provision for including appendixes is not ubiquitous among all sponsor guidelines. For those sponsors that do allow for appendixes, the purpose is generally to provide additional information, diagrams, lists, vendor estimates, and other materials inappropriate for inclusion in the narrative. Each appendix should be labeled at the top of each document to specify what information it contains (e.g., key personnel résumé, bibliography, letter of commitment, etc.). The following list of appendix items shows the various types of documents typically found in appendixes or attachments.

- Bibliography
- Resumes
- Letters of commitment
- Letters of support
- Gantt chart outlining project activities and schedule (if space is unavailable to include this in the narrative)
- Assessment reports showing qualitative and quantitative evaluation results from previous projects related to the current grant project
- Flowcharts illustrating partnership involvement
- Workflow diagrams detailing sequential work to be performed
- Photographs of facility and/or collections to show preservation issues, need for proper storage, or unique content

ⓖ Prepare the Table of Contents

The National Endowment for the Humanities, a major sponsor of library-related projects, consistently requires inclusion of a table of contents within the proposal package. It also should be included, if space allows, in nongovernment proposals containing multiple sections of narrative, budget, and appendixes that exceed ten to twenty pages. A table of contents can be a lifesaver for reviewers during their individual review process. It allows for a central location to make notes that refer to issues they may want to recall in preparing their written comments. During the review panel discussions, reviewers can easily locate sections of proposal packages if a table of contents is available. Even more importantly, it gives reviewers a sense of completeness of the proposal package, to the degree to which the table thoroughly identifies its content. Lastly, because of the large volume of grant submissions for each funding opportunity, one of the biggest challenges facing reviewers is being able to remember application content strengths and weaknesses during deliberation. If a table of contents is well prepared, it can serve to trigger a reviewer's recollections of a proposal's strengths or uniqueness.

The table of contents usually begins on the first page of the narrative (after the abstract) and includes primary and secondary section headings within the narrative. It continues using a cumulative page numbering system to include the budget, budget narrative, appendixes, and other attachments in the order in which the sponsor has directed within the guidelines.

The table of contents may include within its appendixes section the list of individuals, organizations, or institutions represented by those who have provided letters of commitment and/or support. Other headings of appendixes may include key personnel résumés, sample media articles, bibliography, and so forth. Each category of appendix item should appear in the table of contents with its corresponding beginning page number. An example of a table of contents, excerpted from an awarded proposal, is available in appendix 6.3.

ⓖ Key Points

Understanding the purpose and methods for preparing required components most often found in grant applications can provide the necessary context for preparing fundable proposals. It is important to remember these key points:

- The order provided by the sponsor for packaging the proposal should not be used as a guide for preparing each component. The preparation of grant proposal elements should begin with the work plan.
- There are a variety of ways to clearly communicate work plan content that depend on allowable space, complexity of the project, and the sponsor's guidelines.
- A budget has the power to reveal the truth about the actual intentions of the applicant regarding the proposed activities to be accomplished during the grant period.
- An information-rich opening paragraph gives reviewers all the basic information about a project to facilitate the application evaluation and deliberation process.
- Even though a project description is not required by the sponsor's guidelines, the project team should determine the best place, within the first page of the narrative, to include specifics about the project's goal and objectives.

- There is nothing more important than including evidence-based information within sections describing the need for or significance of a project.
- Using a logic model framework frequently is required as a means of conveying grant project evaluation plans.
- Ensure that activities related to a project's evaluation also appear in the work plan.
- Letters of commitment are very different from letters of support in that commitment letters include a description of the role the letter author agrees to perform, as well as his or her endorsement for the proposed project.

The next chapter sets out "dos" and "don'ts" for writing and packaging proposals.

⌬ Appendix 6.1: Sample Statement of Significance

(Excerpt from "Early American and British Children's Literature Digital Collection: A Full-Text Digital Collection for Research, Teaching and Public Programming" authored by Suzan Alteri, Bess de Farber, Chelsea Dinsmore, E. Haven Hawley, Laurie Taylor, and David Van Kleeck, 2015: 9. The Institutional Repository at the University of Florida. http://ufdc.ufl.edu/AA00032859/00001.)

The Significance of Children's Literature as a Research Area

Historical children's literature has played an important role in contributing to the holistic view and understanding of culture, and in supporting academic by-products of literature, history, and cultural studies. In 1932, French philosopher Paul Hazard argued that England could be reconstructed entirely from its children's literature. The texts encapsulate perspectives of what it means to become a member of society at particular moments in history, and their study by scholars shapes notions of how politics, religion, class, race, gender, and other aspects of national culture are formed by individual development. *Pilgrim's Progress*, published in 1678, was not a book written for children; rather, Bunyan and later writers like Maria Edgeworth, Lewis Carroll, and others provide glimpses into the past, and about the values and practices of people in their time. What a society chooses to print and produce for children illuminates cultural norms and self-perceptions; and what a society prints to inculcate social values and identity in children reveals important aspects of what it means to belong and participate in that culture. Major cultural discussions, such as ideas of citizenship and civic duty, empire and expansion, and how to educate children, often occurred and were played out in children's literature texts and periodicals. Early American and British children's literature texts contributed to the invention of the modern idea of childhood and the formalized body of children's literature, as well as to concepts of what a young reader's relationship to larger society should be.

Children's literature printed or published during the early American and British periods consisted of catechisms (both religious and non-religious), moral education, textbooks, hymns, travelogues, fairy tales, fables, and history, with indistinct boundaries between nonfiction and fiction. In Great Britain, children's literature became a notable subset of the book market by the mid-eighteenth century. Thomas Boreman published titles for child readers beginning in 1730, and John Newbery commenced his successful children's book business in 1744, publishing works intended to delight and instruct, such as *Little Pretty Pocket-Book*. Although often focusing on religion, education, and morals,

British publishing contained fiction, such as *Robinson Crusoe* and *Gulliver's Travels*. By contrast, the majority of children's literature in early America served didactic purposes, and fairy tales printed in America did not compete with highly sought titles such as *The Pilgrim's Progress*, *The New England Primer*, and *A Token for Children*.

Considered one of the most significant works of early British literature, *Pilgrim's Progress* illustrates the shift from importation to cultural adaptation in the Anglo-American book trade. Scholars consider *Pilgrim's Progress* a "children's" book less for its content than because so many editions were published specifically for children during the eighteenth and nineteenth centuries. Not originally written for children, Bunyan's text quickly became a key literary work for Puritans. Ruth MacDonald's 1985 assertion that to many immigrants knowing of *The Pilgrim's Progress* was a mark of acculturation into American society remains a touchstone for recent scholars. *The Pilgrim's Progress* featured prominently in classics of American literature such as *The Adventures of Huckleberry Finn* and *Little Women*, proving its enduring appeal as an acculturation device for the literate.

During the Colonial period, readers procured *Pilgrim's Progress* through imported editions and domestic production, with the first US edition originating in Boston in 1681. Over a century later, Isaiah Thomas printed *The Christian Pilgrim*, an abridgement of *Pilgrim's Progress*, as the first US edition specifically for children in the US. The Baldwin Library has 21 different editions of this title from 1755 to 1823, with 12 printed or published in what is now the US, 9 from Great Britain, and 2 imitations penned by Mary Martha Sherwood and printed in Great Britain (*The Infant's Progress* and *The Indian Pilgrim*). The puzzles formed by overlapping titles and adapted content illustrate the transatlantic connections of the early American publishing market, trends in printing technology, and the rise of both the publishing industry and the children's book market. Most American editions were published as *The Christian Pilgrim*, however an 1806 edition of *The Christian Pilgrim* appears in Great Britain, demonstrating two-way influences in trade. In the US from 1790 to 1823, printers often acted as publishers by distributing their products to other booksellers, shops, and printers. By comparison, John Newbery established his successful publishing firm in London by 1744. Other similarities remained, such as apprenticeships as a route for establishing new printing concerns addressing demand for children's literature.

The universe of interested audiences for early American and British children's literature is expansive because of the multi- and interdisciplinary nature of children's literature and printed books from 1630 to 1823 (See Appendix E [note: in original source]). Beyond scholarly communities, children's literature from this time period has been used in K–12 classrooms, religious and social instruction, homeschooling, museums, and other cultural heritage institutions. However, research in early American and British literature and history continues to grow, with 32 prominent academic journals dedicated to this time period. Many of these journals, such as *Early American Literature*, *New England Quarterly*, *Eighteenth-Century Studies*, *ELH: English Literary History*, and the *History of Education Quarterly*, include articles featuring children's literature or childhood studies. Within the fields of children's literature and the history of childhood, five peer-reviewed journals regularly publish articles on historic topics, with *Children's Literature Association Quarterly*, *Children's Literature*, and *Journal of the History of Childhood* most significant in the US.

Scholarly publication on children's literature in the early American and British periods can be traced back to the mid-19th century, with current research taking on topics ranging from citizenship, national identity, and social values to fairy tales, gardening, and trauma. Scholarship produced with support from Baldwin Library materials shows a variety of approaches, topics, and research areas. Representative recent academic books include: John Demos, *The Heathen School: A Story of Hope and Betrayal in the Age of the Early Republic* (2014); Paula T. Connolly, *Slavery in American Children's Literature, 1790–2010* (2013); and Courtney Weikle-Mills, *Imaginary Citizens: Child Readers and the Limits of American Independence, 1640–1868* (2012). Scholars regularly publish articles in peer-reviewed journals and present research at conferences and symposia of the Modern Language Association (MLA), the Children's Literature Association (ChLA), SHARP (Society for the History of Authorship, Reading, and Publishing), and the Society of the History of Childhood and Youth (SHCY), among others. Recent major articles include Sara L. Schwebel, "Childhood Studies Meets Early America," *Early American Literature*, 2015; Lucia Hodgson, "Infant Muse: Phyllis Wheatley and the Revolutionary Rhetoric of Childhood," *Early American Literature*, 2014; and Megan A. Norcia, "The London Shopscape: Educating the Child Consumer in the Stories of Mary Wollstonecraft, Maria Edgeworth, and Mary Martha Sherwood," *Children's Literature*, 2013. (See Appendix F [note: in original source].)

⑥ Appendix 6.2: Sample Budget Narrative Document

Grant Period: January 8, 2014 to September 23, 2014

Personnel ($13,540)—Funding is requested for effort related to planning and executing the proposed project by the project team as follows: Principal Investigator Michele Tennant, Ph.D. (.025 FTE totaling $...........); Co-Principal Investigators include Mary Edwards, Ed.D. (.10 FTE totaling $...........); Hannah Norton (.10 FTE totaling $...........); and Nancy Schaefer (.10 FTE totaling $...........).

Student Labor ($1,793)—100 hours @ $10/hour for a graduate student to support two Collaborating with Strangers Workshops, including promotion and recruitment of participants, workshop preparation and assistance, post workshop survey input and analysis, development of online network group component, and communication. 100 hours @ $7.93/hour for an undergraduate student to update VIVO records and assist with adding materials to the Institutional Repository.

Fringe Benefits ($3,644)—Fringe rates were calculated as follows: 26.3% for faculty librarians, and 4.6% for student labor.

Contracted Services ($2,500)—Formal evaluation of project CoLABs, as well as aspects of instruction, the workshop and the open access publishing fund will be completed by Dr. M. David Miller, Professor of Research and Evaluation Methods in the College of Education at the University of Florida.

Collection Materials ($2,500)—The project team will work with partners to identify important one-time purchases of materials related to women's health and the gender/sex differences in medical research. Materials in digital formats will be preferred over those in print.

Open Access Publishing ($10,000)—The project team will work with members of The University of Florida Open Access Publishing Fund, managed by Smathers Libraries' librarians, to award UF faculty, post-doctoral researchers or graduate students with support to open access journal publishing related to women's health and the gender/sex differences in medical research. Awards will range from $750 to $3,000 depending on the request for publication fees, type of journal, or number of authors. Availability of these funds and subsequent awards will be promoted widely. The project team will evaluate applications based on set criteria to be developed, that best support the project theme.

Honorarium—($500)—Keynote speaker for the workshop to be held at the University of Florida will be offered a $500 honorarium.

Parking Fees—($199)—Parking fees will be paid for non-UF attendees at the workshop held at the University of Florida.

Travel ($10,779)—Members of the project team plan to disseminate the project's activities and results at six annual conferences to be expensed as follows: Tennant will attend American Society for Human Genetics, San Diego, CA, October 2014 ($700 registration; $650 airfare; other expenses will be paid by the HSC Library). Schaefer will attend the Florida Public Health Association Annual Educational Conference—location and dates not yet decided ($190 registration; lodging for 3 nights—$200/night; $270 car rental and gas for 3 days) and the Special Libraries Association Annual Conference, Vancouver, Canada, June, 2014 ($714 registration; $700 airfare; lodging for 4 nights-$300/night; $100 taxi). Edwards will attend the Medical Library Association in Chicago, IL, May 2014 ($395 registration; $531 airfare; lodging for 4 nights—$200/night; $35 taxi). Norton will attend the Institute for Healthcare Advancement, Health Literacy Conference in Irvine, CA, May 2014 ($359 registration; $625 airfare; lodging for 4 nights—$125/night). Garcia-Milian will attend Society for Neuroscience, Washington, DC, November 2014 ($660 registration; $500 airfare; other expenses will be paid by the HSC Library). Keynote speaker for workshop held at UF ($1,250 for airfare, lodging; keynote not yet determined).

Indirect Costs ($4,545)—This represents 10% of direct project costs. (Tennant et al., 2013: 25)

⊚ Appendix 6.3: Sample Table of Contents Document

     (Jefferson et al., 2014)

⊚ References

Alteri, Susan, Alan Rauch, and Bess de Farber. 2014. "Women Authored Science Books for Children 1790–1890: An Annotated Bibliography." The Institutional Repository at the University of Florida. http://ufdc.ufl.edu/AA00027007/00001.

Caswell, Thomas, James Cusick, John Nemmers, and Bess de Farber. 2011. "Unearthing St. Augustine's Colonial Heritage: An Interactive Digital Collection for the Nation's Oldest City." The Institutional Repository at the University of Florida. July 20. http://ufdc.ufl.edu/AA00004298/00001.

Clapp, Melissa, Bess de Farber, Barbara Hood, Margeaux Johnson, and Ann Lindell. 2011. "Collaborating with Strangers (CoLAB) Grant Proposal." The Institutional Repository at the University of Florida. March. http://ufdc.ufl.edu/AA00013651/00001.

Covey, Stephen R. 2004. *The 7 Habits of Highly Effective People: Restoring the Character Ethic.* New York: Free Press.

Doran, George T. 1981. "There's a S.M.A.R.T. Way to Write Management's Goals and Objectives." *Management Review* 70, no. 11: 35. Business Source Premier, EBSCO*host*.

Hines, April, and Bess de Farber. 2011. "Collaborating with Strangers In and Outside Mass Communications." The Institutional Repository at the University of Florida. http://ufdc.ufl.edu/AA00019151/00001.

Jefferson, Rebecca, and Bess de Farber. 2012. "The Florida Digital Newspaper Library: Broadening Access and Users." The Institutional Repository at the University of Florida. March 16. http://ufdc.ufl.edu/AA00010438/00001.

Jefferson, Rebecca, Bess de Farber, John Nemmers, et al. 2014. "Repositioning Florida's Judaica Library: Increasing Access to Humanities Resources from Florida, Latin America, and the Caribbean Communities." The Institutional Repository at the University of Florida. http://ufdc.ufl.edu/AA00022790/00001.

Knight Foundation. 2015. "Knight News Challenge: Winners: How Might We Leverage Libraries as a Platform to Build More Knowledgeable Communities?" September 23. https://www.newschallenge.org/challenge/libraries/evaluation.

McAuliffe, Carol, Bess de Farber, and Stephanie Haas. 2009. "From the Air: The Photographic Record of Florida's Lands: Phase III." The Institutional Repository at the University of Florida. March 9. http://ufdc.ufl.edu/UF90000014/00002.

Nemmers, John, and Bess de Farber. 2009. "Saving St. Augustine's Architectural Treasures." The Institutional Repository at the University of Florida. http://ufdc.ufl.edu/UF00094090/00001.

Reakes, Patrick, Margarita Vargas-Betancourt, Bess de Farber, Myra Torres Alamo, and Laurie Taylor. 2012. "Florida and Puerto Rico Digital Newspaper Project: National Digital Newspaper Program (NDNP)." The Institutional Repository at the University of Florida. January 15. http://ufdc.ufl.edu/AA00019344/00001.

Simpson, Betsy. 2009. "Shifting Patterns: Examining the Impact of Hiring Non-MLS Librarians." The Institutional Repository at the University of Florida. November 25. http://ufdc.ufl.edu/UF00095937/00001.

Taylor, Laurie N., Bess de Farber, Haven Hawley, et al. 2015. "Digital Humanities Collaboration Bootcamp—Full Catalyst Grant Application." The Institutional Repository at the University of Florida. http://ufdc.ufl.edu/AA00028978/00002.

Tennant, Michele, Mary Edwards, Hannah Norton, Nancy Schaefer, and Rolando Milian. 2013. "Sex and Gender Differences / Women's Health Outreach Project." The Institutional Repository at the University of Florida. http://ufdc.ufl.edu/AA00019464/00001.

CHAPTER 7

Grant-Writing Tips and Potential Errors to Avoid

THIS CHAPTER PRESENTS A COLLECTION of recommendations for ensuring that a proposal is well received by reviewers. Because writing and preparing grant proposal packages is different from other types of writing, it is important to be aware of what works and what does not. Proposals written by novice grant-writers often can be easily identified during the review process, and this can hurt a proposal's chances of being awarded. The overall intent of a proposal is to cumulatively build the reviewer's confidence in the applicant's project quality and capacity to complete the project successfully within the grant period. If for some reason the quality of the proposal is compromised, then of course the reviewer's confidence is likely to be diminished.

Writing Suggestions

Affirmative Verbs

Grant applications, by their nature, are presenting information about activities that will take place in the future. Unfortunately, writing in the conditional tense gives the reviewer a sense that the applicant may be uncertain that activities will occur as described. Words such as "should," "could," "would," or "may" can contribute to a perception of insecurity, or a lack of commitment. They tend to weaken any case for support or any plan to execute a project, and therefore should be avoided whenever possible.

Some grant-writers may feel that using active verbs such as "will" presents an inaccurate image of the future. During the project team's discussions, questions may arise that can prevent them from being assertive about planned activities or project results, such as:

- How can anyone be certain that this project activity will happen in year two?
- What if those technology changes and the equipment proposed become obsolete during the grant period?
- What if the partnering organization experiences personnel turnover affecting the project result?
- What if a proposed library event gets rained out?

None of these types of questions or concerns about the future of proposed activities should inhibit grant-writers from using affirmative verbs throughout every proposal narrative. The more uncertain the language, the less likely reviewers will feel confident about the project and its applicant.

Here is an example of how uncertainty can creep into a proposal. Suppose a librarian is requesting funds for the purchase of ten iPads for short-term loans to students and faculty. The librarian knows that the library hosts classes for a few professors. Rather than using the conditional verb to suggest that students attending these classes "would" be able to access the iPads, the librarian should emphasize that the project "will" make these tablets accessible to students in classes hosted by the library, and that professors "will" be informed about how to reserve tablets to ensure their awareness of this opportunity. If the librarian is uncertain that students will have access to the iPads during classes hosted by the librarians, then this information should be excluded from the proposal.

Pronoun Usage

It can be quite annoying for a reviewer to have to read proposals loaded with pronouns. The overuse of pronouns such as "we," "our," and "I" can turn a perfectly good proposal into a monotonous and confusing document. Consider the issues that might arise when using the pronoun "we." The project being proposed identifies several different groups: the project team with only members from the applicant library, on-campus partners, and external organization partners. In this case, if the writer uses "we" to identify only the project team members, and the reviewer assumes "we" is being used to identify all participants, then confusion results. Each of these groups should be defined by the writer and consistently used throughout the proposal to ensure the reviewer is not making incorrect assumptions.

Overusing "our," for instance, creates other issues. It prevents reviewers from branding the application with the name of the applicant organization or the title of the project. Consider the situation that occurs if all applicants use "our" in their narratives. How difficult will it be for reviewers to recall which applicant applied for which project?

When writing proposals for fellowship opportunities (grants to individuals versus organizations) applicants often use "I" throughout their narratives. Imagine the degree of monotony this might create for reviewers. Those applicants that invest time in devising alternate ways of presenting information about themselves in these types of proposals often pay more attention to other details within their applications that make them stand out among the competition.

Appropriate Tenses

Writing in the appropriate tense can be challenging. The problem with ambiguous or inconsistent tenses that arises for reviewers is that it can be difficult to discern whether activities described in the narrative already have occurred, are occurring while the application is being prepared, have not yet occurred but will occur prior to the grant period, or that the activities will take place during the grant period for which the applicant is applying.

Consider the case where a librarian is requesting funds to collaborate with a software developer. The developer already has been testing the software prior to working with the librarian. While the librarian is preparing the application, the developer and the librarian are collaborating on training library users to test the software. The partners also are planning additional testing prior to the grant period. During the grant period they plan to expand the project to train new groups of students, create tutorials, and codify the software for wider distribution.

Writing the narrative for such a project will require consistent reference to time frames and the use of the correct tense to describe activities. For instance, in this case if the developer is describing the project in the present tense, because many of the software developments already are functional, then reviewers may wonder why an application was submitted for work that already has been completed. Essentially, the problem is that grant-writers prepare applications months in advance of the actual review process. If this factor is ignored during the proposal preparation period, then it is likely that the narrative will not specify time frames, will use incorrect tenses, and may thereby ultimately confuse reviewers.

Identifying the project's many phases can provide some remediation. The librarian can describe current activities under the heading of startup phase, planning phase, or phase I. Activities that will take place prior to the grant period can be described as project testing phase or phase II. And activities planned during the project grant period can be identified as the implementation phase or phase III. For reviewers, this shows a progression of activities that strengthens the proposal. It gives the librarian credit for all the work that has occurred previously and that will occur prior to the grant period. Such a proposal gives reviewers increased confidence in the collaborators. The proposal provides evidence of their combined investment of time and effort, which produces a proposal that poses fewer risks than other "new" projects.

Generalities, Superlatives, and Salesmanship

If the goal of the library applicant is to create a mental movie of the project, then the lack of detailed information provided in the application will inhibit this desired result. A declination, if it occurs, should result from reasons other than a lack of proposal specificity. If you have a great idea and paint an invisible picture on the application canvass, then the idea has no value.

The same holds true for applicants who feel the need to sell their project by using language that generalizes and exaggerates the quality of the project, its history, and past results. A phrase such as "The website has been overwhelmingly successful at serving patrons" provides no evidence of traffic to the website. Or consider this phrase: "Past presentations have been popular beyond the team's expectations," which lacks a definition for popular, and the team's original expectations may not be relevant to reviewers. These statements lack any credible evidence. In fact, the Andrew W. Mellon Foundation's grant proposal guidelines state "that the Foundation expects concision and few, if any superlatives in proposal narratives" (Andrew W. Mellon Foundation, 2014: 1).

Words such as "some" or "many" only leave reviewers with questions about how many. These words may indicate that the applicant library lacks statistical information about its programs, and its patrons and audiences served.

Another offense, often committed by novice grant-writers, is the use of salesmanship. Consider the situation where a proposal narrative briefly describes a project in general terms and then populates the next few pages with the project's potential benefits to various constituent groups. The reviewer hasn't been able to grasp the full description of the project and instead is being bombarded with information about all of its various benefits and potentially wonderful results. The truth may be that the librarian feels insecure about the quality or eligibility of the proposed project and, instead of providing a feasible description, is trying to use up valuable real estate by elaborating on the project's benefits.

Another example of salesmanship is when the project title alludes to the creation of a model for others to follow, without having completed a proof-of-concept or pilot project. In this situation, the applicant is trying to convince reviewers that a new idea, yet to be tested, is such a terrific idea that simply funding its initial activities will automatically result in an exemplary project for others to replicate. In this case, rather than including the word "model" in the title, the applicant can posit that, if successful, a result of the initial project will be a model for other libraries to follow. To strengthen the potential "model" aspect of the proposal, the applicant can propose to produce and widely distribute a step-by-step guide of how to replicate the project as part of the project's activities work plan and dissemination plan.

Librarians should use restraint when it comes to using superlatives and salesmanship. Instead, providing attendance or website usage statistics, testimonial language quoted from a survey, interview or letter of support, or other factual information allows the library's project team to take full credit for its level of success. The facts will speak for themselves—in volumes.

⊚ Tips for Professionalizing the Presentation

Use the Entire Grant Period

The sponsor's guidelines will include the date that funding will become available to start a new project, and the end date by which all funds must be expended. This is known as the grant period. A common mistake made by novice grant-writers is not to use the entire grant period to the project team's advantage. For instance, the project may be a festival to showcase a library's services. The project team plans to present a scavenger hunt for patrons of all ages to learn about the library's collections and to meet its librarians. The event will take place on July 10 and 11. The project team may determine that the start of the project should be July 1 and the end date should be July 30. One month seems a reasonable amount of time to start and complete the project. But the guidelines may state that projects must be no longer than one year, beginning January 1 and ending December 31.

The project team actually is shooting itself in the foot by not taking advantage of the entire year as offered by the sponsor. Selecting a shorter time frame tells the reviewers that the team is inexperienced and may be overly optimistic. There's so much more that can be accomplished with this type of project if given a year to execute a more sophisticated plan, which might include building an online scavenger hunt, video-recording contestants for uploading to the library's YouTube presence, and other ideas for marketing and promoting the event and the collections themselves. One month doesn't allow for fully planning, coordinating, promoting, evaluating, and sustaining methods for exposing a library's collections to its local community and to the world.

Granted, if the sponsor offers three-year grant periods, the project team should determine the adequate amount of time necessary to complete the project, which may be less than two years. In almost all cases, the project team should not elect to complete projects in less than one year if a year is the grant period offered by the sponsor.

Use Headings That Match the Sponsor's Guidelines

Within the sponsor's guidelines you will see a variety of headings for separating the narrative content. These headings usually match up with one or more criteria for evaluating the proposal. Mirroring the headings provided in the guidelines helps reviewers easily find where the proposal content is located. If most of the applicants use the same or similar headings, as outlined in the guidelines, then the reviewer's job will be more streamlined and time efficient.

Another approach to this straightforward method is to be inventive and create your own headings. Yes, this will set you apart from the field of competing proposals. Some applicants change the headings to make them correlate with the project idea. Or they believe the application will be boring to reviewers who have to read the same headings over and over again.

But being inventive with headings may send some other messages or create questions for the reviewers, such as:

- Is this the applicant's first grant application submission?
- Where's the advantage in creating unique headings?
- Why didn't the applicant read the guidelines?
- Is the material in this section going to answer the narrative questions presented in the guidelines?

Inserting too many headings also can be an unfortunate option; not only has the applicant mirrored the headings contained within the guidelines, but every few paragraphs the application presents additional headings ostensibly to assist the reviewers. This strategy can convey too much information. During the evaluation process, reviewers match the narrative content to the guidelines, not to the ideas presented in the proposal. A few additional headings may be just right. But going beyond can show an applicant's insecurity or inexperience.

The worst alternative would be to eliminate all headings. This can occur if the applicant runs out of space and decides to remove all the headings, thus generating more space to complete the narrative. Or, it may be that the applicant assumes that reviewers know what narrative content is required and have no need for headings.

Removing all the headings simply gives reviewers headaches. Try to visualize a road map to get from your house to Guatemala without the advantage of demarking the cities, highways, states, and street names. It can be done, but the experience will be painful.

Use Headers, Bullets, Numbers, White Space, and Hyperlinks

These structural enhancements to narrative content can go a long way in helping reviewers in their task of evaluating your proposal package. Inserting a header that includes the title of the project and the name of the applicant library, or parent institution applicant associated with the library, helps to remind reviewers of the applicant without having to turn to the first page of the narrative. Every page of the application package benefits by identifying the applicant and title in the top right corner. As the reviewer turns each page, he or she can see the name of the applicant organization and be reminded of the project title.

This is particularly important when applicants choose to refer to the project as "the project" rather than using the title or a portion of the title throughout the proposal. It is best to try to infuse the project title throughout the proposal narrative. If this isn't possible, then the information included in the header may suffice.

Using bullets or numbers helps to break down complex descriptions of a project idea and other components of the narrative. It is particularly helpful when outlining the project's SMART goals and objectives; in describing plans for project activities, evaluation, or promotion; or for identifying the various types of audiences that the project plans to attract or serve.

Cramming too much information into a proposal by eliminating all the white space can be very hard on the eyes. Reviewers need the benefit of white space whenever it can be included.

Using hyperlinks is one way to create more space on the page. It gives the applicant the option of allowing existing online content to speak on behalf of the applicant. Now that proposals are ubiquitously submitted to sponsors electronically, hyperlinks should be used as a tool to embed additional contextual information in the proposal. Hyperlinks can

- substitute for long descriptions of partnering organizations;
- point to bibliographic references or personnel profiles when appendixes are not permitted;
- showcase web pages that include descriptions of collections, past event promotional materials, or library guides;
- feature photographs of deteriorating collections or facilities; and
- highlight video clips of conference presentations, instructional sessions, or tutorials.

Pay Attention to Real Estate

Narrative content is expected to be unbalanced. Most of a proposal's real estate should be used to describe the project and its significance, impact, or the need to be addressed. Guidelines vary widely. Some will specify the number of pages, or the number of words or characters for describing specific sections in the proposal. Others will simply provide the maximum number of pages to be used in order to complete the narrative. In this last instance, the applicant must pay attention to the length of each section to ensure the content takes into account the reviewers' needs for sufficient information.

For instance, a dissemination plan that is longer than three-quarters of a page may be preventing the adequate description of the evaluation plan, which is only one-quarter of a page—due to a lack of available space. This could be because the project team has strengths in marketing and promotion, but lacks know-how in project evaluation methodology. A proposal should try to remedy this type of disparity. The bottom line here is to use the available space wisely in order to ensure that the reviewers have sufficient information to determine the degree to which evaluation criteria have been met.

Tell a Story

From a reviewer's viewpoint, stories are welcome additions to any proposal. Telling a story can be the most effective way for reviewers to learn about a collection, a project's needs, or the potential for raising matching funds. When reviewers feel satisfied that a proposal has enlightened them in some way, especially unexpectedly, then the project team has achieved an enviable result.

For instance, the National Endowment for the Humanities Challenge Grant Program, initiated in the 1970s, is a unique federal program that provides applicants with the opportunity to request $1 for every $3 in new funds raised for an important humanities-related fund-raising project. It might be for the purpose of improving facilities for humanities collections or endowing a new humanities position in a library. The best way to compete for these matching awards that each average $500,000 is to convey the story behind the development of the humanities need or opportunity, the timing for the fund raising effort, and the potential for successful funding initiatives. Reviewers must feel compelled to support the project in the same way that donors who are made aware of the fund-raising campaign will become convinced of the project's future impact on the humanities, and decide to contribute to the cause.

Stories should be filled with facts to create the fullest impact on the reviewer. They should contain some surprising and unexpected details that reviewers will be grateful to learn. And they should build cumulatively from one enlightening piece of information to another.

Methods for Avoiding Common Errors

Making Assumptions about the Reviewers' Knowledge

Reviewers are most often strangers to the applicants, except in the case of private foundations where sometimes reviewers are working collaboratively with applicants in the development of the project and budget. Government sponsors may share the names of reviewers or describe typical characteristics of those who will be selected to complete the review process. Board members of major foundations are often those who serve as reviewers. For United Way and community foundations, reviewers are sometimes members of the board of directors or community representatives. For local government and CRA funding, reviewers are typically county commissioners, or boards represented by a mix of commissioners and community representatives.

To ensure that reviewers completely understand all aspects of your proposal, it is best to write proposal narratives from the viewpoint that reviewers are completely unfamiliar with the project, including its partners, personnel, technology, and budget. Taking this approach prevents applicants from inadvertently making reviewers feel unprepared or at the very least, confused. It also prevents reviewers from making erroneous assumptions about the project.

Reviewers are entitled to have the opportunity to completely and thoroughly understand a project's content. But if the applicant uses acronyms, technical terms, jargon, and other shortcuts, then it puts the application at risk of being difficult to understand. It also may appear condescending to the reviewers.

Specialized language works well when the applicant is absolutely certain that all the reviewers are versed in the same language. For instance, if a librarian is applying for a Project Ceres grant award allocated by the U.S. Agricultural Information Network (USAIN), it can be assumed that specialized language related to libraries and agricultural collections would be acceptable. The USAIN members evaluating proposals are knowledgeable about this specific field.

But the same logic does not apply to applications for the Council on Library and Information Resources Hidden Collections Programs. The reviewers for this program are likely to be a mix of scholars from a variety of disciplines, not necessarily librarians. Reviewers for the National Endowment for the Humanities also are quite diverse in their backgrounds, geographic roots, and expertise.

An effective antidote to apply so as to avoid making assumptions about the reviewer's knowledge is to have a non-library professional read the proposal. Have the reader ask you as many questions as he or she can about the project; you'll see how much clarity of language is missing from the proposal. The outside professional's questions should be viewed as a gift and accepted with grace without defensive posturing. Rewriting these sections will elevate the quality of the proposal.

Presenting Narrative Content Chronologically

Another challenge for novice grant-writers is to describe a project without using a chronological framework. The problem often arises when a librarian has been integrally involved in the project's development over a period of a few years. Because so much has occurred from the time the project began, the librarian believes there is much to communicate to reviewers. To explain this complex project, some librarians may feel obligated to take a chronological approach to describing the project. In this situation, the librarian may think that it is impossible to convey the project description without first describing its entire history, including all project activities, issues, participants, decisions, and rationale presented in an organized manner chronologically so as to prepare reviewers for learning about the proposed project.

If this has been your strategy, then it is important to work to overcome the impulse of telling all. Application guidelines form the container for all narrative responses. If the first section of the narrative instructions does not include a "Project Background and History" section, then this information should not be imparted until later in the proposal, if the guidelines provide a provision for including the project's history. Not all guidelines include a project history section.

This means that the librarian and the project team must practice describing the project as it will look in the future, beginning the first day of the funded grant period. To get credit for all the previous planning, testing, activities, events, partnerships, and personnel efforts that came prior to the grant period, the project team will need to determine where some of the most important slices of the project development story will fit best. When the project team prefers to impart a complete chronological description, this preference should raise a red flag. Of course, if a chronological representation is prescribed by the guidelines, then these recommendations would not apply.

Abusing or Ignoring the Appendixes' Content

The inclusion of appendixes is not universally allowed. Check the guidelines to find a provision for appendix items. Also, verify the types and file size limitation for digital content of items that are acceptable for inclusion in the appendixes.

Problems can arise when appendixes are populated incorrectly. This scenario provides an example. The guidelines require a work plan or an evaluation plan, but you have failed to reserve sufficient space in the narrative to include this content. As a remedy, your project team opts to include the required narrative section as an appendix item. They may rationalize this strategy by determining that the application will not be penalized for being "incomplete." Although this may be a correct assumption, consider the reviewers' point of view here. Suppose that all of the other applicants have included the work plan in the narrative as instructed, and your application is the only one where reviewers must hunt for the work plan or the evaluation plan within the appendixes. This takes extra time and can easily cause frustration.

These situations arise when applicants find themselves trapped by a narrative that is too long. Making the decision to cut portions of the narrative for inclusion in the appendixes can be dangerous. Reviewers expect to see required narrative material in the prescribed narrative section. Appendixes are intended to supplement the narrative with additional information. They are not intended to substitute for required narrative content.

Regardless, whatever content gets delegated to the appendixes should be referred to in the narrative. You might have all kinds of terrific visual or informative content within the application appendixes that none of the reviewers will ever see. Imagine spending hours finding, formatting, labeling, and organizing this section without a plan to motivate reviewers to go there. A solution is to refer to the specific or applicable appendixes whenever possible.

For instance, you have quoted from a letter of commitment in the narrative. Take the opportunity to add: "(see Letter of Commitment, appendix B)." Or the project team has secured estimates from vendors for converting microfilm to digital content. Make sure to include a statement such as "(see Vendor Estimates, appendixes A, B, and C)" within the budget narrative section. And in the case where you have attached the Gantt chart as a visual representation of the narrative work plan, then you should add "(see the Gantt chart, appendix F)" at the end of the work plan narrative.

Finally, too many documents—such as more than three letters of support, résumés for those other than key project personnel, or excessive numbers of reports—can make your proposal package look and feel like overkill. If the proposal itself has insufficient merit, then regardless of the volume of appendix items, it will be declined. Your choice of what to include or exclude in the appendixes will contribute to showing your respect and consideration for the reviewers charged with evaluating many applications. Keeping the reviewers' needs in mind throughout the proposal preparation process will contribute immeasurably to your efforts to create fundable proposals.

Strategies for Editing, Securing Approvals, and Packaging Proposals

Librarians generally do not allot sufficient time for editing, securing approvals, and packaging proposals. As service providers, librarians and library project team members are often preoccupied serving patrons and other types of customers. Being unable to predict a typical day's workload makes it challenging to commit enough time to edit, secure approval signatures, and package applications for submission. Multiply these challenges by the number of collaborating partners involved in the proposal submission process (such as time needed by partners to secure cost share commitment letters as required by their academic institutions), and you'll find that the challenge may appear to be insurmountable.

The first recommendation is to block out at least four days prior to the deadline for these purposes. Making appointments with copyeditors and approvers well in advance helps to segregate the necessary time to complete these tasks. Why do you need four days?

(1) Editing, making corrections, and rereading a full grant proposal can take time and multiple iterations in working with a variety of people. For instance, the budget if prepared by an accountant should be reviewed by the project team and the accountant's supervisor. The narrative should be read aloud slowly to most efficiently catch grammatical errors. A copyeditor should review a penultimate version for consistency in terms of tenses, project description content, time frames, and formatting, as well as typos, punctuation, and spell-checking. Also ensure that margins and font sizes meet the sponsors' requirements by sharing these specifications with your copyeditor. Such activities will take longer than one day to complete, especially if each collaborating partner also is charged with reviewing a penultimate version.

(2) Seeking approvals can be a lengthy process, especially if an approver wants to read the entire proposal. If this is the case, then be prepared to add time to make the required changes offered by the approver(s).

(3) Packaging the content of a proposal can take at least one full day. Federal grants require submission using http://www.grants.gov, and include the completion of forms that will require time to prepare. Additionally, time is needed to check the pagination of the proposal content, create the table of contents if applicable, and label the appendixes so that reviewers will easily be able to identify each appendix item.

For instance, if a résumé is included for the project director, then this label, "Project Director," should appear at the top of the résumé. If the appendix item is a letter, it should be labeled at the top as "Letter of Support" or "Letter of Commitment." Each appendix item should be labeled at the top of the page. Because these items may be PDF documents, Word or Excel documents, or screen shots, they each will require time to format and label. Adding page numbers to the entire proposal also will consume time. Once the page numbers are added, the entire document should be printed and verified along with the table of contents to ensure accuracy. Errors may occur at any time during this packaging process, so make sure you reexamine all content after completing this process.

The packaging issue of entering information into an online application format is important to address. Rather than simply uploading file attachments for each application component, these online applications require that the applicant type or cut and paste directly into prescribed delimited containers. An applicant should not assume that the space limitations for the number of words or characters within these online applications match up with their own content calculations. Sufficient time should be allocated to test space availability when cutting and pasting content into online containers, or uploading files or images restricted by size.

Since the advent of the Internet for widely promoting the availability of grant opportunities, compounded by the ease by which proposals can be submitted electronically, competition for grant funds has risen and continues to grow. The increase in applications has impacted reviewers' evaluation processes. Finding reasons to eliminate an applicant early in the review process allows reviewers more time to focus on those applications that are complete, well organized, well edited, and professionally presented. These indicators, which are readily discernable, can send messages to reviewers that the applicant respects the process, and the time that reviewers will invest in their evaluation.

Consequently, regardless of how many hours have been invested by a project team and its collaborating partners in preparing all of the various components of the application package, it is worth investing at least four days to complete your team's editing, approving, and final packaging activities. Doing so will contribute to a more gratifying experience for your future grant reviewers.

Key Points

It is important to consider how the quality of the written proposal package will impact the reviewers. Remembering these key points will produce a proposal of professional quality.

- The grant period can be used as a guide to ensure that the narrative tense is appropriate to the time frame being discussed.
- The use of proper names instead of pronouns allows the project team to brand the applicant and the project title in the reviewers' minds.
- If you can assume that the reviewers know nothing about your project, this helps ensure that you will provide them with all the necessary information to evaluate your grant proposal.
- The appendixes section should only be populated with items that add value to your presentation, and referencing these in the narrative can contribute to a cohesive application package.
- Reviewers need to be oriented throughout the grant application presentation to show that the applicant has followed the guidelines and respects the reviewers' contributed time and efforts.
- The project team should reserve at least four days to finalize content, seek approvals, and complete the sponsor's remaining application requirements. This time frame will prove to be invaluable in achieving the team's goal of submitting a proposal package that is nothing less than excellent.

Employing the collaborative grant-seeking guidance in this book will contribute to the possibility of exciting new learning and pioneering grant awards for your library and your communities. Perhaps you have never attempted it, or maybe you have years of grant-seeking experience. Regardless, the journey into grantsmanship can happen at any time. The practice of grant-seeking is certain to become more prevalent and important in libraries. As this discipline continues to evolve, grow, and mature, your participation can make a profound contribution to improving people's lives. Just imagine the future opportunities for philanthropic grant funding that the aging baby boomer generation will create. The future looks promising; the adventure awaits. . . .

Reference

Andrew W. Mellon Foundation. 2014. "Grant Proposal Guidelines, The Andrew W. Mellon Foundation: Scholarly Communications." October 6. https://mellon.org/media/filer_pub lic/24/e0/24e0b0e7-c8a3-4b2a-983f-decfacb8e26a/grantproposalguidelines_sc100614.pdf.

Index

corporate sponsors, 66; Chipotle, 66; Office Depot, 66; Starbucks, 66; Target, 66

cost share, 29, *31*, 36, *38*, *40*, 50, 57, 78, 79, *90*, *92*, 105, 107, 108, 119, 138. *See also* contributed effort; in-kind contribution(s)

Council on Foundations, 65, 72

Council on Library and Information Resources, 65, 136

cover sheet, 30, *31*, 39, *40*, 57, 58, 82, 94

creativity, 11, 15, 20, 21, 100

criteria, 7, 18, *19*, 27, 28, 29, 32, 38, 39, *40*, 42, 43, 44, 56–58, 81–84, 86, 88, 91, *92*, 100, *103*, 113, 125, 133, 135. *See also* evaluation criteria; review criteria

database(s), 62, 68–71, 80, *92*

deadline(s), 8–10, 16, 17, 19, 26, 28, 37, 39, 42, 48, 56, 59, 62–64, 68–70, 75, 76, 79–82, 84, 88, *92*, 94, 100, 114, 138; master deadline schedule, 70–72

declined, 29, 38, 42, 45, 48, 51, 82, 86, 87, 89, 90, 101, 137

dissemination plan, 99, 113–15, 132, 134

eligibility, 28, 57, 63, 66–68, 132

eligible, 6, 17, 25–27, 29, 57, 63, 66, 67, 80–82

errors, xii, 7, 129, 135, 138

evaluation criteria, 28, 32, *92*, 113, 135

evaluation plan, 90, 115, *116*, *117*, 118, 122, 134, 137

evidence, 33, 39, *40*, *43*, 58, 86, 88, 94, 95, 113, 119, 122, 131, 132

examples of proposals awarded by external sponsors, 48–50, 54–56, 59, 60, 102–4, 108, *116*, *117*, 119, 124–27; *Collaborating with Strangers*, 102, 119, 126; *Collaborating with Strangers In and Outside Mass Communications*, 119, 126; *Digital Humanities Collaboration Bootcamp*, 110, 111, 127; *Early American and British Children's Literature Digital Collection: A Full-Text Digital Collection for Research, Teaching and Public Programming* (pending review), 122–24, 126; *Florida and Puerto Rico Digital Newspaper Project*, 108, 119, 120, 127; *Florida Digital Newspaper Library: Broadening Access and Users*, 54, 55, 60, 116, 127; *From the Air: The Photographic Record of Florida's Lands: Phase III*, 104, 127; *Repositioning Florida's Judaica Library: Increasing Access to Humanities Resources from Florida, Latin America, and the Caribbean Communities*, 55, 56, 60, 108, 125–27; *Saving St. Augustine's Architectural Treasures*, 102, 103, 127; *Sex and Gender Differences / Women's Health Outreach Program*, *117*, 124, 125, 127; *Shifting Patterns:*

Examining the Impact of Hiring Non-MLS Librarians, 127; *Unearthing St. Augustine's Colonial Heritage: An Interactive Digital Collection for the Nation's Oldest City*, 50, 101, 102, 114, 115, 126; *VIVO: Enabling National Networking of Scientists*, 48, 49, 59

examples of proposals awarded by internal library grantmaking programs, 48–60; *Analyzing Librarian-Mediated Literature Searches in the Health Sciences*, 52, 60; *Creating a National Juried Selection Process for an Artists' Book Collection (ARTBOUND)*, 51, 52, 60; *GatorScholar: Developing a Database to Foster Interdisciplinary Communication and Collaboration*, 48, 49, 60; *Historic St. Augustine Block and Lot Files*, 50, 59; *Ian Parker Collection of East African Wildlife Conservation*, 52–54, 60; *Moving Forward!—A second-phase project to digitize anniversary issues of the legendary American Jewish newspaper the "Forverts" ("Jewish Daily Forward"): a special sub-collection within the Price Library of Judaica Anniversary Collection*, 54, 55, 60; *A Performing Arts Approach to Collection Development*, 55, 60; *The Price Library of Judaica Anniversary Collection: A First Project to Digitize a Unique Set of Jewish Newspapers*, 54, 59

expenses, 6, 8, 18, *19*, 24, 30–32, *41*, *43*, 46, 57, 58, 66, *81*, 106, 107, 114, 120, 125; allowable, 6, 66, 82, *92*, 106, 107, 121; consultant(s), 29, *31*, 32, 46, 78, 79, *93*, *103*, 106; disallowable, 6, 66, 82; equipment, 8, *31*, 32, 34, *37*, *38*, *41*, 46, 58, 81, *92*, 102, *104*–6, 120, 130; indirect costs (IDC), *92*, *93*, 96, 107, 120; other, 106, 125; outside professional services (OPS), 33, 36, 38, 46, 57, *92*, 106; personnel, 31, 32, *38*, 58, 85, *92*, 102, 105, 124; salary(ies), 29, 36, 85, 105, 106; supplies, 28, *31*, 32, 37, 38, 41, 58, 66, *92*, 102, 106; travel, 2, 28, *31*, 46, 47, 58, 79, *81*, 87, *92*, 106, 114, 125; vendors, *41*, 78, 79, *92*, 106, *116*, 137

facilities, xi, xii, 11, 23, 46, 62, 63, 72, 76, 84, 95, 134, 135

feasibility, 15, 28, 37–39, 42, 77–80, *92*, *93*, 95, 100

fellowship(s), 63, 87, 130

foundation(s), 7, 61, 64–70, 87, 100, 113, 115, 132, 135, 141; Andrew W. Mellon Foundation, 67, 68, 72, 132, 139; Bank of America Charitable Foundation Inc., 65; community foundation(s), 65, 69, 87, 135, 141; Ford Foundation, 64; Gates Family Foundation, 64; GE Foundation, 65; John D. and Catherine T. MacArthur Foundation, 64; Knight Foundation, 109, 127; Robert Woods Johnson Foundation, 64; United Way(s), 65, 87, 115, 135, 141; W. K. Kellogg Foundation, 64;

About the Author

Bess G. de Farber has been the grants manager at the University of Florida Libraries since 2008, and previously served in the same position at the University of Arizona Libraries. She has provided grantsmanship instruction throughout the past twenty-seven years for audiences including graduate-level library and information students, as well as arts, museum, and social service agency professionals; and she has led efforts to secure millions in grant funding for nonprofits and academic libraries. Her research interest is asset-based collaboration development. As a certified professional facilitator through the International Association of Facilitators, she invented Collaborating with Strangers Workshops, under the umbrella of CoLAB Planning Series, which are large-group-facilitated processes for individuals and organizations seeking new collaborative partnerships. This process has served more than six hundred organizations and 1,800 individuals since 2002.

De Farber has served on grant review panels for the National Endowment for the Arts, Florida Division of Cultural Affairs, Education Foundation of Palm Beach County, Arizona State Technology Research Initiative Fund, and the Children's Trust in Dade County, Florida. As a program officer for the Community Foundation of Palm Beach and Martin Counties, and also for the Palm Beach County Cultural Council, she managed the allocation of over $10 million in grant funds for arts and culture, human and race relations, and social services. De Farber has served as a consultant to numerous organizations including the Children's Services Council of Palm Beach County, Morikami Museum and Japanese Gardens, United Way agencies, and Community foundations. She holds a master of nonprofit management degree from Florida Atlantic University, and a bachelor of music degree from the University of Southern California.